"Kevin Treston asserts correctly that teachers work in one of the most stress-related fields. For this reason, teachers need to nourish themselves and replenish their commitment, energy, and creativity. *Five Dynamic Dimensions for Effective Teaching* provides teachers with a refreshing tool for re-examining and re-committing themselves to their vocation. If I were a principal, I wouldn't hesitate to use this book as a resource for faculty inservice."

Joe Paprocki
Catechetical Consultant,
Archdiocese of Chicago
Author, *Empowering the Catechist* and
Tools for Teachers

"There are certain qualities fine teachers share that set them above the pack, that make them memorable for years afterward in the minds of those they teach. Kevin Treston, an experienced and gifted teacher, here examines five qualities that he feels are essential to the good teacher. He explores in depth the qualities of integrity, wisdom, generativity, learning, and justice, and shows how each of these adds the special dimension that enhances a teacher's overall ability to reach her or his students.

Perhaps most important of all, he emphasizes the need for teachers to take time for themselves. He recognizes how busy teachers are—full-time schedules or part-time volunteering can put strain on family life and time for personal growth. By insisting that teachers make time for themselves and cherish it, he performs a great service for harried, over-tired teachers everywhere."

Deborah McCann
Columnist, *Religion Teacher's Journal*

"This book provides an in-depth look at 'teacher' as person, as educator, as learner, as role model, as provocateur, and as a source and nurturer of wisdom. We strongly recommend it for personal reading, inservice days, faculty meetings, teacher-to-teacher use and discussion groups. If you're looking for one book that has the information you need to help you become a great teacher, this is it!"

Dr. Janaan Manternach
Dr. Carl Pfeifer
Authors, *Creative Catechist*

"This book provides an opportunity for teachers to reflect seriously on their vocation through five lenses—integrity, wisdom, generativity, learning, and justice—each in itself a central dimension of teaching, which, taken together, form a rich kaleidoscope of the totality of teaching.

Treston combines theory with illustrations from Scripture, the writings of others, and from life itself, all of which bring vitality and relevance to his basic message. I particularly appreciated the reflection questions at the end of each chapter which help bring the topic home to that reader who is seriously processing the chapter's content.

Any person who teaches—in the broadest definition of the term—will be helped by this book."

Kenneth Stokes
Executive Director,
Adult Faith Resources
Minneapolis, MN

F • I • V • E
Dynamic Dimensions
for
EFFECTIVE TEACHING

Kevin Treston

TWENTY-THIRD PUBLICATIONS
Mystic, CT 06355

Acknowledgments

I wish to thank a number of people who have helped me with the composition of this book. First, thanks to Kathryn for her support in writing; to Tim Keating, Alana Osborn, and Paul McCann for their invaluable critical suggestions; to Rob Cosgrove for his careful editing and helpful advice. I thank, too, all my colleagues in Brisbane Catholic Education, especially those in Faith Education Services for all I have learned from them.

Scripture quotations are from the *Jerusalem Bible* published and copyright 1985 by Darton Longman and Todd, Ltd. and Doubleday and Company, Inc. and used by permission of the publishers.

Twenty-Third Publications
185 Willow Street
P.O. Box 180
Mystic, CT 06355
(860) 536-2611
800-321-0411

ISBN 0-89622-716-2
Library of Congress Catalog Card Number 97-60104
Printed in the U.S.A.

Dedication

I dedicate this book to all teachers, especially to the teachers who have influenced my life: my mother and father as my first teachers; my family; Mr. Reg Goodman, my primary school teacher; to the Marist Brothers for sharing their rich heritage of education; and all other teachers in the various programs I have undertaken.

In particular, I dedicate this book to my dear brother Neville as he struggles to recover from a horrific car smash. His suffering has been a poignant teacher to our family and friends.

May those teachers who read this book experience support, affirmation, and challenge in their vocation.

Brisbane 1995

Contents

INTRODUCTION

This book is intended to assist all those who teach in schools, parishes, and other educational agencies.

The motives people have for becoming teachers are extremely complex. During many seminars with teachers, I have been fascinated by the stories of teachers who tell how they arrived at their decision to enter the teaching profession or become catechists. Their stories suggest that people decide to become teachers for a variety of reasons that range from altruism, economic prospects, a sense of a Christian vocation to teach, following the example of family members who are teachers, to "not-sure-but-give-it-a-go" motives.

Although many of the examples given in this book are drawn from a school environment and teaching children and adolescents, I believe that the basic issues explored in the text—integrity, wisdom, generativity, learning, and justice—are highly relevant to any context of teaching, such as parish adult learning groups.

Today, thanks to a whole series of movements in our society, teachers are experiencing increasing stress. The impact of dysfunctional families and consumerism, the influence of economic rationalism on teaching policies and curriculum, and the challenge of communicating the Christian story in a secularized environment are just some of the forces that can erode the morale of teachers. The community is understandably sensitive about educational issues that relate to its most precious resource: its children. There is a public perception of falling standards of education. Teachers may also feel that their status in the community is in decline. Adult religious educators may find it difficult to entice people into participation in the face of the allure of media entertainment, stressful life situations, overscheduling in people's lives, and church censorship of controversial topics.

Five Dynamic Dimensions for Effective Teaching describes the enterprise of teaching from five perspectives. There are many other aspects that I might have used for explanation but I have chosen these because of their contemporary relevance. The perspectives of integrity, wisdom, generativity, learning, and justice reflect five essential dimensions of teaching. Each quality reflects the values and practices that highlight the essence of good teaching. The five qualities are situated within a Christian context of education with special reference to the wisdom of Jesus the Teacher. Although the general orientation of the book is a reflection on teaching within a school or college context, much of the content of the book is applicable to all teachers, including pastors and adult religious educators.

Before discussing these qualities I would like to reflect first on what it's like being a teacher.

On Being a Teacher

Once upon a time there was a school. The religion teacher asked a small boy this question:

> "Johnny, can you tell me who made you?"
> Johnny answered immediately, "God made part of me."
> His teacher replied, "What do you mean 'made part of you'?"
> Johnny responded, "Well God made me little and I growed the rest myself!"

While we might question Johnny's theology, we can certainly endorse his emphasis on growth as a cooperative venture between himself and others. Teachers know that students learn only what they choose to learn. Teaching aspires to be a reciprocal activity between teachers, students, family, church, curriculum, and other social influences in the community. Good teaching seeks to develop a student's potential by using all the positive influences that teachers themselves have learned through continued education. Teaching is the art of partnering with others who seek the well-being of students. This movement from independence to interdependence as a cooperative venture requires both the acquisition of skills and a paradigm shift in teaching styles.

The contemporary teaching landscape is being reshaped by many social forces, such as the breakdown of social cohesion, cultural diversity, consumerism, and the impact of electronic technology. Teachers can no longer maintain the status of remote authority figures but are accountable to parents as well as to the bureaucracies that employ them. The threat of litigation is a shadow across every school. Teachers can sometimes feel that they are becoming technical functionaries within an impersonal bureaucratic system. The level of frequency of student violence against teachers is steadily rising. Even the relative autonomy of teachers in their classrooms is being undermined by cooperative teaching. Research has shown a sense of frustration among teachers from a loss of status and respect in the community. The generally poor media profile does not help the teacher morale. There is a strong expectation of partnership between parents and teachers, industry and schools. Within church circles, the conservative wing of the church looks with a jaundiced eye on some religious education programs in the schools and parishes.

As a teacher you may wonder about the many roles you are expected to perform. Are you a representative of the parents with the students? Are you a public servant? A carrier of the cultural tradition of society? An employee of the state or church school system? A missionary? A political or social engineer? A facilitator of learning? A counselor? A representative of the teaching church? Teachers perform many diverse roles. Sometimes they may feel that, in any one school day, they engage in all these roles, in addition to the various roles of family member, parish member, and member of the wider community! Teachers in schools and parishes are asked to respond to a host of societal and church demands on their emotional, spiritual, and psychic energies.

However, the flip side of these issues affirms teaching as a worthwhile vocation. While teachers may feel besieged by pressing concerns, they are also a resilient group motivated by deep conviction in what they are doing to help students. Many teachers have strengths that have a lasting influence on their students. Such teachers are enthusiastic about education and they stimulate learning through their knowledge and love of their subjects. Their genuine care for their students is an affirming presence. They celebrate the enthusiasm of people who discover the richness of biblical spirituality in the parish Scripture classes. I certainly remember with prayerful gratitude the many teachers who have shaped my values and encouraged my commitment to life-long learning. Mr. Reg Goodman, my primary school teacher in a little rural school in a sugar cane district in North Queensland, Australia, showed me the power of self-learning as well as communicating specific knowledge; Maria Harris at Boston tapped into my creativity; John Dunne at the University of Notre Dame revealed the profundity and mystery of one's life journey; my mother showed me the gift of positive thinking; my father, a farmer, shared his love of the earth with me.

Teaching is more than a communication of knowledge. It is also a revelation of self, the sharing of a trustful presence which pervades every facet of the dynamics of teaching. What matters most in teaching is not the mechanics of the interchange of ideas but the power of the teacher's values and expertise to transform the hearts and minds of those engaged in the experience of teaching and learning. Such a process of transformation happens within the context of a respect for the individual freedom of each student and a passion for holistic learning to happen. Good teaching seeks to instill in students a love of learning. Teachers can be strengthened in their work if their teaching emanates from a worldview that is in accord with the dream of Jesus: "I have come so that they may have life and have it to the full" (Jn 10:10). As teachers, we hope our students will not only develop skills to make a living but will also learn how to live creatively and morally.

We may never know when someone catches a dream from us!

Many years ago I heard a story about a teacher that made a lasting impression on me. Here it is:

Once upon a time a king wished to discover and honor the greatest person in his kingdom. Finally, after many months, a number of prominent people were assembled in the palace courtyard. The king sat on his throne and each person was brought forward as the court attendant read out to the assembly the list of achievements of that person.

A very wealthy merchant was first presented, then a woman with extraordinary healing powers, a prominent church leader, a governor of a province, and a lady who worked with lepers. As each person was presented to the king, it was clear that choosing the greatest person was going to be a very difficult task.

Finally an old lady was called forward. Her hair was white, her face wrinkled but glowing with love and the wisdom of her years. The king asked, "What has this woman done to deserve the honor of being the greatest in my kingdom?"

The master of ceremony replied, "My lord, you have seen and heard all the others. This woman is their teacher."

At once, the king rose from his throne and applauded this woman. He invited her to come forward and as she knelt before him, he crowned her as greatest person in his kingdom.

The five dimensions presented in this book propose five essential aspects of a teacher's vocation. I have no doubt that many other qualities could be specified, but I believe that the fostering of these five personal qualities will enhance the quality of teaching. I have chosen to situate these qualities within a Christian vision of education.

Integrity is the way of inner truthfulness; *wisdom* enables a teacher to discern and communicate authentic ways of living; *generativity* empowers a teacher to choose life for self and propose life choices for students; *learning* is the effective facilitation of learning; *justice* is the pursuit of action to promote a more harmonious world. To foster these qualities is to choose to be learning companions with students on journeys of life and faith.

Let us now explore the first quality: integrity.

1

INTEGRITY

My first impressions of her were not favorable. She disturbed our complacent teacher meetings with her incisive questions and ability to name accurately what was happening. My inclination was to smooth over the evident differences between the staff members. Not Felicity! With great honesty she would insist on clarifying the issue under discussion and articulating her position, even if it was unpopular with the group. Gradually I came to admire her integrity and acknowledge her contribution to a culture of openness among staff at meetings. Felicity's actions reminded me of a story about truthfulness.

Once upon a time in a land called Is, there lived two tribes. One tribe was known as Truth and the other as Untruth. In the beginning all went well because everyone knew which tribe they belonged to. However, as time passed, the people began to get confused about which tribe they belonged to. You see, if you asked a person from the tribe of Truth which tribe she belonged to, she would answer, "To the Truths." But if you asked the same question to a person from the tribe of Untruth, she would answer, "To the Truths" because she always lied. After many years the confusion got worse because the people began to intermarry and the children inherited a bit of truth and untruth. Eventually everyone was a mixture of truth and untruth.

One day a stranger came to the land of Is. The stranger was pure truth although no one recognized him. He always spoke the truth. When he saw someone doing good he praised this person. Likewise, when he saw evil, he would tell them so, not because he wanted to hurt them, but because he loved them and he never lied. You see, he hoped that by so doing, he would root out untruth.

The people of Is who heard about the truth in them were thrilled but the others who were told about evil became furious. The stranger, who had come to heal and bring people to truth, became a cause of division and anger. In the end, the people of Is were unable to face their own truth. They gathered together and killed the stranger who was truth.

The Meaning of Integrity

The story of the people of Is illustrates that the first essential dimension for a teacher is integrity. This quality is concerned with our inner truthfulness, the affinity between our core values and our behavior. Integrity enables teachers to act according to the deepest desires of the heart. Questions such as, "What do I live for?" "What do I value?" "What is my vision of life?" "What kind of person do I aspire to become?" challenge us to ground our behavior in discerned values. Principle-centered teaching leads to security and wisdom because we are true to our beliefs in our relationships with ourselves and our students. The inner peace of integrity is a solid foundation for action.

Many teachers live at a bewildering pace. During any one working day they may be involved in a wide range of activities, such as classroom teaching, speaking with parents, coaching sports, schoolyard and bus supervision, pastoral care, interaction with peers, attending meetings, administrative duties, preparing supper for the family before conducting the sacrament program in the parish, etc. Although the variety of situations may evoke a wide spectrum of responses, such as giving encouragement, providing information, listening, and challenging student behavior, integrity anchors the responses in our core values and beliefs. Teachers can more confidently act on particular issues if they are in touch with their own charter of beliefs.

Teachers demonstrate their integrity when they are resolute in upholding stances that are congruent with their values, even though their actions may sometimes conflict with personal convenience. After all, sometimes it is easier to be dishonest and avoid personal embarrassment. A teacher may feel the pulls and tugs of the dilemma of choosing a course of action that is authentic for him or her but will probably provoke criticism or worse. Without integrity we become easy prey for passing ideologies. There is an old saying: "If you don't stand for something, you will fall for anything."

A teacher's salary is a necessary component of the work of teaching. Teachers, like the rest of the community, have to pay bills and mortgages. But teaching is not just another job for material ends. It is hoped that the profession of teaching is first of all a vocation to communicate lifelong values to students. A life of integrity enables teachers to share a vision of life that promotes our identity as daughters and sons of God in partnership with the earth. Teachers who courageously align their behavior with guiding principles provide students with healthy role models in an age of cynicism. Integrity reflects our character and flows from a habitual belief in the worth of every single person and thing.

Integrity is the fruit of fidelity to the inner life of the Spirit. We do not possess integrity as a static thing. Our joys, traumas, angers, laughters, loves, and hates are springboards to our quest for ultimate meaning within a faith stance. Through attending to the lessons of our life experiences, we may gain insight into what we really believe and not what our fantasies suggest. If we hope to reach a measure of inner truthfulness which is in the mind of Christ, then we long for the abundance of God to transform the seasons of our life journeys. Paul's prayer in Ephesians expresses this hope, "In the abundance of his glory may he, through his Spirit, enable you to grow firm in power with regard to your inner self, so that Christ may live in your hearts through faith, and then planted in love and built on love, with all God's holy people you will have the strength to grasp the breadth and the length, the height and the depth; so that, knowing the love of Christ, which is beyond all knowledge, you may be filled with the utter fullness of God" (Eph 3:16–19).

Psychologist Carl Jung reminds us that "we meet ourselves in a thousand disguises along the way." The ebb and flow of our life experiences invite us to appreciate our human vocation to be faithful stewards of creation. The evolutionary nature of the way of integrity is illustrated by the words of Catherine of Siena who said "the way to heaven is heaven." In the same vein, Jung wrote, "wholeness is not completion but perfection." We descend into the depths of our integrity by interiorizing the events of each day through the lens of faith and grace. Stephen Covey, author of *The Seven Habits of Highly Effective People*, speaks about the "inside-out" approach whereby people operate from an intentional and interior value stance.

The path of integrity does not imply any comfortable arrival at an end point but rather living with the unfolding stories of the ambivalence of relationships. We struggle to embrace and befriend feelings of loneliness as well as intimacy; we wrestle with anger as well as enjoy laughter with friends. The authenticity of our integrity depends to some degree on how well we incorporate the shadow of failure into our worldview. An essential element in the development of our integrity is our willingness to learn from our mistakes and sinfulness. We struggle to make sense out of conflicting ideas and the paradox of competing demands on our quest for a path of integrity. Some days teachers can feel on top of the world. Other days suggest there is a giant plot to make our days as teachers as miserable as possible. A disruptive class manages to sabotage a brilliantly planned lesson. The DRE in the parish has double-booked the hall and you find that your morality class is locked out. We forget a vital appointment with the school principal or DRE. We come to the awful realization that report cards were due in yesterday and not next week as previously thought. And just when we have sought the refuge of home for respite, one of our children reminds us that we are expected to attend the school music festival! The downsides of teaching are opportunities to embrace all the dimensions of our experiences, not just the pleasant ones. The Zen saying, "When my barn burned down, I could at last see the moon," illustrates the truth of the potential for learning from the things that don't work out for us.

The sense of incompleteness in our quest for an authentic life can generate in us an esteem for the spirit of truth. As teachers, we aspire to be honest in our dealings with our students. We apologize when we are guilty of injustice. When we don't know, we say so. We recognize that we are never really able to grasp and contain Truth, but we learn from its unfolding wisdom in our encounters with the seasons and passages of life. Integrity is grounded in the realism of who we really are and not on the illusion of someone we pretend to be.

The Greek word for truth is *aletheia*, meaning to unveil, to uncover that which is hidden. Integrity moves us beyond outward appearances to savor inner truth. There are many addictions or compulsions, such as the accumulation of material possessions, power for power's sake, and pleasure, which can divert us from the pursuit of a wholesome life. We recall the warning of St. Augustine: "They go ahead to admire the heights and mountains, the mighty billows of the seas, the course of the rivers, the vast extent of the ocean, the circular motion of the stars, and yet pass themselves by" (*Confessions* 10, 8). We need to cross over the moats of illusions of self to reach the inner castle of truth. For religious people, a vibrant spirituality is a driving force toward a life of integrity.

Integrity and Self

To relate creatively to others requires, first, that we nurture life-enhancing values within ourselves. Many years ago Plato wrote, "Self-knowledge would certainly be maintained by me to be the very essence of knowledge and in this I agree with him who dedicated the inscription, 'Know thyself!' at Delphi" (Plato, *Charminides*, 164B). The following Taoist story from ancient China illustrates the theme of "know thyself":

When Yen Ho was about to take up his duties as tutor to the heir of Ling, Duke of Wei, he went to Ch'u for advice. "I have to deal," he said, "with a man of depraved and murderous disposition. How is one to deal with a man of this sort?"

"I am glad," said Ch'u Po Yu, "that you asked this question. The first thing you must do is not to improve him, but to improve yourself."

If we have a clear self-awareness, we are able to discern the motivation for our decisions—whether our efforts for career promotion are driven more by ego needs and economics than by something really true to ourselves or the organization. Shakespeare wrote in *Hamlet*:

This above all:
To thine own self be true;
And it must follow,
as the night the day,
Thou canst not then be false to any man (Act I. III).

The problem with "to thine own self be true" is that we easily deceive ourselves about our motives. The eminent philosopher and biologist Charles Birch has written, "It is too easy to kid ourselves about what is the true self. We need to discover what we think we are and rise above that. And for that we need an image of the human that goes beyond what we are. For Christians this is what they see Jesus and those who reflect him to be" (Birch, 171).

On the same theme, one of my best friends shared with me this reflection which he discovered in his mother's prayer book after her death:

When you get what you want in your struggle for self, and the world makes you king for a day, then go to the mirror and look at yourself and see what the guy has to say. For it isn't your father or mother or wife whose judgment you must pass. The fellow whose verdict counts most in your life is the guy staring back from the glass. He's the fellow to please, never mind the rest, for he's with you clear up to the end; and you have passed your most dangerous, difficult test if the guy in the glass is your friend. You may be like Jack Horner and chisel a plum, and think you are a wonderful guy, but the man in the glass says you're only a bum if you can't look him straight in the eye. You can fool the whole world down the pathway of years, and get pats on the back as you pass; but your final reward will be heartaches and tears if you've cheated the man in the glass (Anonymous).

Integrity is the hallmark of the great teachers of history. When we think of teachers such as Socrates, Confucius, the Buddha, and Jesus, we are in awe of their influence on our civilization. Then there are a host of teachers throughout the centuries who have enlightened us and expanded the scope of wisdom. I think of Hildegard of Bingen; Anne Sullivan, who guided the hands of Helen Keller; Hans Christian Andersen, the teller of fairy tales; Mary MacKillop; Jean Vanier; Mary, the teacher of Jesus; and Nelson Mandela, who taught us lessons of reconciliation.

People of integrity are women and men of extraordinary courage because they have to ride out the storms of ridicule and criticism as well as let go the power of their own ego needs. In my life, I have been inspired by the integrity of the Jesuit Teilhard de Chardin who suffered the pain of being ostracized by representatives of the official church. One glimpses the character of his own truthfulness in his writings about the search for the interior life. In his book, *Le Milieu Divin*, Teilhard describes his inner journey:

> For the first time in my life, perhaps, although I'm supposed to meditate every day, I took the lamp and leaving the zone of everyday occupation and relationships where everything seems clear, I went down into my innermost self, to the deep abyss whence I feel dimly that my power of action emanates. But as I moved further and further away from the conventional certainties by which social life is superficially illuminated, I became aware that I was losing contact with myself. At each step of the descent, a new person was disclosed within me of whose name I was no longer sure, and who no longer obeyed me. And when I had to stop my exploration, because my path faded beneath my steps, I found a bottomless abyss at my feet, and out of it came—arising I know not where—the current which I dare call my life (Teilhard de Chardin, 76-77).

We face many challenges when we commit ourselves to a life of integrity. We constantly make choices about how we will respond (or not respond) to structures, regulations, and systems that limit human dignity. As an employee in a particular system or church, we may sometimes feel we are walking a tightrope between loyalty to the system and concerns for justice. How one is both loyal to the employing agency and subversive for justice is a painful dilemma for teachers of integrity. Entrenched power brokers can punish those who rock the institutional boat.

Teachers in schools and parishes are just one group among the many educators in society. The family is the primary teacher of values although the media increasingly shapes the values of the community. Other formative influences include the local and global community, computerized technology (internet), the church, and our earth. In this era of societal upheaval and explosion of knowledge, there is a growing concern that many people are losing their psychic and spiritual roots through a loss of a common social vision. Social commentators describe the *angst* of people who suffer from a sense of alienation and a disintegration of a cohesive meaning system.

Having a Philosophical Map

It is imperative that teachers work from a coherent philosophical map that reflects the values of being fully human (Jn 10:10) and created in the image of God (Gn 1:27). Our philosophical map illustrates the contours of our beliefs and the route we follow in what we teach and how we teach. During a staff in-service day, I remember being involved in a rather animated discussion with a teacher who was dismissive of raising philosophical issues about learning. He argued strongly that we should be concentrating on "real" issues. One thing is certain in teaching. Whether we are aware of it or not, we all have a philosophy of teaching that provides the direction of our teaching. By examining and critiquing our assumptions about teaching, we are in a better position to modify them if this seems beneficial. The "Reflection" exercises at the end of this chapter will assist you in clarifying the contours of your own philosophical map.

Western society is characterized by technological sophistication but lacks an inherent meaning system. But without a philosophical foundation how can we ensure that technology serves the well-being of the communal cycle of the earth community? Anthropocentrism, that is, a belief that all creation is made for the benefit of humankind, is a particularly destructive ideology because it presumes that the myriad forms of creation have no other identity than to serve the consumerist whims of people. Technology has contributed greatly to humankind, but its powers of persuasion are formidable. Our consciousness is significantly shaped by a technological society that generates images of life-styles and cultures. We can become so immersed in a consumerist culture that we fail to critique the images of the "good life" from the gospel imperative to be faithful disciples. A technological culture propagates the message that a country's basic goal is to maximize economic growth, that progress is measured by the strength of the gross national product, and that technology will itself inaugurate a reign of bliss.

People are presented with an array of options as to what to eat, drink, wear, and how to be entertained. Yet many people live in a state of anxiety and stress. We hear so much about sustainable economies but who talks about sustainable life-styles? The cult of individualism endorses a view that happiness is found in self-fulfillment. Individualism conflicts with a Christian vision, which promotes sustainable life-styles within the context of the principle of the common good. Our destiny is not to live in a state of alienation from the world but by sharing the joys, wonders, and heartaches of the life of the earth community.

The power of the life of one truthful person cannot be underestimated. I recall attending the funeral of a humble shoemaker who touched the lives of so many people by his friendliness and willingness to repair shoes, even if they could not pay. After the funeral Mass, I heard stories about Jim's goodness and care for anyone who entered his shop. A helpful exercise is to imagine our own funeral and listen to what people will remember most about our life. What is the heritage we wish to leave behind? The story of Alfred Nobel is instructive. In 1912, he was shocked to read his own obituary in the local newspaper after his death was mistakenly reported. The obituary described Nobel as one who devoted his life to making weapons of war. Nobel was determined to do something about this commentary on his life. We now acknowledge his contribution to peace through the annual Nobel Peace Prize.

In order to recognize our own integrity, we need personal space to distance ourselves from our cultural conditioning. Sabbath time helps us to develop perspectives on the values and personal expectations that drive our actions. Every day teachers make instant decisions about the facilitation of learning, time management, priorities between family and school, discipline procedures, pastoral care, professional stories, and times for relaxation. Habits of personal reflection or interiority enable us to act from the inner freedom of an intentional value stance. Teaching cannot be reduced to a sterile communication of facts or furthering the goals of education as a business industry. Authentic decisions in teaching flow from specific beliefs about the nature of a human person and our religious faith. Teachers may find the following questions helpful as a focus for understanding their own worldviews:

• What are the most important values I wish to live by?
• How do I act if I believe that every person is loved by God?
• What do I hope are the fruits of my teaching?

- How do I establish esteemed values in my class-room, my school, my parish?
- What do I wish to be remembered for?

One of the most moving stories in the gospels is surely the description of the last moments in the earthly life of Jesus. His life was slipping away in the racking pain of the crucifixion. But even in the horror of his last agony, he announced the completion of his mission, his life work:

After Jesus had taken the vinegar, he said:
"It is accomplished"
and bowing his head
he gave up his spirit (Jn 19:30).

His faithfulness to the way of integrity had led him to this terrible place, but he did not stumble in his fidelity to the mission of proclaiming the Good News of the reign of God. This rather poignant statement about the way of integrity is complemented by the joy of celebrating a faithful life. Jesus expressed the fruits of loving relationships with God by his discourse at the Last Supper: "I have told you this so that my own joy may be in you and your joy may be complete" (Jn 15:11). Truthfulness has its own brand of humor!

To assist you as a teacher in appreciating your own value stance on education, the next section briefly examines some of the ways in which education has been understood throughout the centuries and how key themes in philo-sophical movements impact on education. By reflecting on the various strands of thinking about education throughout the ages, you might be better able to articulate your own philosophical map.

Historical Perspectives on Education

The word "education" evokes many connotations. We may think of education in the formal or informal sense. Formal education is planned and structured and usually is conducted in some kind of schooling or adult program mode. However necessary the structures for formal education may be, this can be a restrictive mode of learning. Much education is informal and happens in almost every facet of society—church, family group, media, and social interactions in the community. Native peoples and Maori cultures integrate education throughout the whole of the life cycle. Education may be considered as time-framed by the length of school and college years or it may be a lifelong process of "birth-to-death" education.

A historical overview of the various aims of education illustrates the diversity of expectations about the purpose of education. The aims of education as stated throughout the centuries cover a wide spectrum—formation for citizenship, vocational expertise, religious and ethical development, personal development, affiliation to political ideologies, and the acquisition of work-related skills. The following statements about education by writers over thousands of years illustrate this diversity:

- Dispelling error and discovering truth. *Socrates*
- Developing the body and the soul of all the perfection which they are capable of. *Plato*
- Leading from the unreal to the real, from darkness to light, from death to immortality. *Upanishad*
- Realization of the illustrious virtue. *Confucius*
- Creation of a sound mind in a sound body. *Aristotle*
- Leading and guiding for peace and unity with God. *Froebel*

- Developing real wisdom. *Erasmus*
- Making life in harmony with existence. *Tagore*
- Fitting the individual to his physical and social environment. *William James*
- Complete development of individuality. *Nunn*
- Development from within. *Rousseau*
- Increasing social efficiency. *Dewey*
- All round drawing out of the best. *Gandhi*
- Developing morality. *Herbart*

These statements may help you express your own understanding of the purpose of education. You will notice that some writers emphasize the role of education as the realization of inner potential. In the history of educational thought, Aristotle, Gandhi, Nunn, Rousseau, and Pestalozzi would represent this view of education. Other theorists, such as Dewey, highlight the role of education as a socializing process for citizenship. Probably your own view of education is a mixture of both schools of thought: education seeks to draw out the potential of students but it is also intended to engage students in religious and communal socialization. If you were asked to sum up your basic view of the purpose of education, what would you say?

A brief overview of the story of education illustrates the complexity of approaches to education because of the diversity of civilizations and cultural aspirations. From the beginning of human civilization, people have learned skills in living, lighting fires, building shelters, and passing on the stories and myths of the tribes. When settlements began to be more consolidated in the Fertile Crescent, the Indus, the Ganges, the Nile, and the Yellow River regions, formal schooling was consolidated. Schools were necessary to transmit written literature and religious traditions, and to impart skills for commercial transactions. Schooling was not for the masses but was restricted to the merchant and upper classes.

Western education was greatly influenced by Greek education. There were many strands of thinking within the Greek heritage. Socrates (469-399 B.C.E.) used questions to elicit further questions, giving birth to ideas already within the listener. His method of scrutiny or enquiry postulated that right thinking is more important than coming to right conclusions. Plato (427-346 B.C.E.) taught that truth may be discovered by reason alone. To gain true knowledge, Plato said that we must leave behind the world of senses and seek by reason the universal *forms* of the intelligible world. Aristotle (386-322 B.C.E.) was more interested in the physical world and proposed that reality is to be found in the world of the senses. The Sophists believed there was no such thing as certain knowledge, but people should strive to attain a successful worldly life. Greek education was oriented toward formation for citizenship and provided an inspiration for the revival of education in the period of the Renaissance.

Roman, Christian, Renaissance, and Reformation education all made significant contributions to the evolving story of schooling, scholarship, and imparting family and religious values. The emergence of the national states during the late Middle Ages and the rise of commercial and scientific societies highlighted the need for education that was relevant to industry. By the middle of the nineteenth century, most western countries were beginning to develop comprehensive systems of education. In our contemporary world the speed of change is so rapid that educators can be almost overwhelmed by the urgency of modifying the goals and curriculum of education. It seems that no sooner do teachers settle into teaching a particular curriculum than another curriculum review is already underway. More than ever before, teachers need to clarify their own charter of beliefs, their own philosophy of education.

Let us examine, ever so briefly, five major philosophies that have had an impact on education. Even these brief statements about each philosophy may encourage you to read more extensively on these philosophies and clarify your own philosophical stance.

Philosophies of Education

The word "philosophy" is of Greek origin, and is made up of two words *phileo* (love) and *sophia* (wisdom). Literally the word means "love of wisdom." Philosophy is the quest for truth and uncovering the mystery of life to make it intelligible. A fundamental question that shapes the culture of every society is, "What does it mean to live, given the fact that one day we will die?" With the evolution of the scientific age, a school of philosophy developed which sought to limit the scope of philosophy to an analysis of sensory experience. For Christian teachers, the scope of philosophy must embrace a search to know self in a relationship with world and God. Christian philosophy of its nature has both a transcendent and immanent character.

The prominent philosophers of history have been concerned about education. Without a coherent philosophy, education would lurch from one transient ideology to another according to the lure of the latest cultural movement. ("Political correctness" is one example.) If teachers are aware of their own philosophical assumptions, they are better able to approach the many challenges to their profession as well as to critique educational trends. Significant educational ideas are distorted when those implementing the ideas do not appreciate their philosophical underpinnings.

Our philosophical standpoint provides a frame of reference for the ways in which we teach and how we choose our priorities in teaching. If our worldview is essentially religious, then the curriculum becomes infused with a religious spirit. If our philosophical position is materialistic, then we offer education that will only provide the skills and expertise to contribute to a personal and communal economy.

The five philosophies described here represent five worldviews of how we construct our meaning system. The tenets of the five philosophies may merge on certain issues but the essential ideas of each philosophy present different visions of reality.

Idealism

This philosophy contends that the spiritual world is the highest realm of reality, superior to the material aspects of our existence. Education based on the philosophy of idealism would encourage students to appreciate the spirituality of being and to come to a knowledge of eternal truths. Such an education would be less inclined to incorporate experiential learning in its teaching approaches, and the scientific world would take a lesser place. Subject matter is very important to education from the perspective of idealism. Teachers would possess a solid body of knowledge and teach this knowledge at depth to students. Idealism has received a boost in recent times as a reaction against the prevailing dominance of pragmatism and economic rationalism in western societies. Plato, Kant, and Froebel would be representatives of the philosophy of idealism.

Pragmatism

Pragmatism focuses on the central place of experience and may be considered more as a method of experimentation than as a philosophy. Unlike idealism, which starts with assumptions about the nature of being, pragmatism focuses on what matters in the here and now. A pragmatic approach to education facilitates a series of learning experiences that are relevant to the social and commercial environment. Values are not eternal but arise out of a continuously evolving world. Truth is a social construct that changes over time. Pragmatic educators have little time for the heritage of tradition unless it illuminates the present. Problem solving, project work, and creative activities are the stuff of pragmatism as applied to education. For Dewey, a chief proponent of pragmatism in education, present experiences are the starting point for the curriculum.

Existentialism

Existentialist writers such as Kierkegaard, Sartre, Heidegger, Jaspars, and Tillich propose that the recognition of individual being is the beginning point of all existence. People are in the process of becoming and have the capacity to freely choose their destiny. Key words that recur frequently in existentialist writings are *freedom, choice,* and *individuality.* Education, according to the existentialists, should assist students to make conscious choices and provide learning spaces for students to explore possibilities for personal development. A caring school environment, pastoral care, and dedicated teachers would help students learn within a network of significant relationships. Students are helped to make choices and decisions. The concerns of students do influence the content of the curriculum. One should note, however, that Christian existentialists would have different starting points in their understanding of human nature from agnostic writers such as Jean-Paul Sartre.

Realism

Realism is not concerned with the world of ideas or spiritual realms but concentrates on the physical world which follows natural laws. Aristotle, an original proponent of realism, pointed out that nothing exists in the conscious that has not first been experienced in the senses. Mathematics and science are esteemed subjects in the curriculum because they better equip students to relate to the physical world and technology. Teaching is considered an organized activity rather than an art. Objectives and outcomes are to be specified. Facts, not opinions, are elicited. Although religious thinking is not fundamentally alien to the philosophy of realism, most realists would tend to regard religion as a by-product of nonscientific minds, which have developed religious dogma as a response to the mysteries of the human condition. John Locke (1690-1781) popularized the philosophy of realism.

Marxism

Karl Marx (1818-1883) believed that our consciousness changes with every modification in the conditions of our material existence. Marx proposed that our minds assume the features of the products we create. Labor is the essence of life, but workers are cut off from their own humanity by having to produce objects owned by others, namely capitalists. When economic ideologies such as capitalism separate humans from the fruits of labor, the result is alienation. This alienation is not just economic separation but personal alienation. Marx advocated a transformation in society that involved the conflict of class struggle so that the dispossessed might control the means of production and distribution. From a Marxist perspective, education is a commitment to class struggle against the perceived forces of oppression. A Marxist system of education is highly central-ized and directs education toward communal rather than individual goals. Religion is to be combated as an enemy of the masses. In the Marxian view, the world is conceived in terms of natural causation and may be manipulated by social revolution. Education should further this social revo-lution in order to inaugurate a just society.

The five philosophies just described have many ideolog-ical faces in contemporary education—the postmodern themes of relativism and suspicion of authority, economic rationalism, futurism and disregard of our cultural heritage, rationalism, and secularism. These ideological faces influ-ence the scope of the curriculum, budget allocations of funding agencies, the shape of teacher formation, parent expectations, and the perceived role of schools in society. As a teacher, you might like to reflect on the philosophical assumptions about education in your school and country. Which assumptions are you comfortable with? Which assumptions conflict with your own vision of education?

Christian Vision of Education

The philosophical influences that impact contemporary teaching theories and practices challenge Christian educa-tors to clarify their own philosophy of education. A Christian philosophy of education cannot be identified with any one school of philosophy. An early Christian principle was quite selective: "take the best and leave the rest." Christian philosophy has adapted ideas from the philoso-phies of idealism, realism, and existentialism but would be alien to the philosophies of pragmatism and Marxism. Idealism and realism both emphasize the place of reason and propose that there is a certain body of knowledge that should be known and communicated to each generation in our culture. Existentialism, if it has a theist orientation, can be aligned with a Christian philosophy of education because it affirms the sacredness of each person and opposes dehumanizing elements in society.

The word "education" in its Latin origins (*educere* and *educare*) suggests the bringing forth of something previously hidden. This developmental feature of education is characteristic of many theories of education, as are the communal goals. The confusion between schooling and education has often muddied the waters of defining the nature and purpose of education. Most education happens outside schools.

A Christian vision of education is founded on the absolute value of a human person, created in the image of God and redeemed by the saving mission of Christ. Christian faith insists on the centrality of the historical figure of Christ as revealing the compassion of God. The teachings of Jesus offer a vision of a reign of God where peace, reconciliation, and love would prevail over the forces of evil. Jesus invited his followers to live in a radically different way through a new community style (*koinonia*) and to see their lives as spent in service toward others, especially the poor (*diakonia*). The mission of the church is to teach (*kerygma*) the Good News of salvation. The story of Jesus is an emphatic affirmation of our humanity: "The Word became flesh, he lived among us" (Jn 1:14).

The contemporary dominance of eco-technical philosophies makes it imperative that Christian educators articulate and communicate a new vision of education that incorporates both the wisdom of its Didache tradition and those cultural movements which are aligned with a holistic appreciation of humankind within a unitary, planetary consciousness—like the scribe in Matthew's gospel, "Well then any scribe who becomes a disciple of the Kingdom of heaven is like a householder who brings out from his storeroom things both old and new" (Mt 13:52). Christian educators will draw insights from their 2000-year-long educational heritage and forge an expanded vision of education that resonates with an evolving collective psyche.

Some cultural movements that offer both challenges and opportunities for Christian educators include: a growing awareness of the feminine (virtually all written philosophy has been postulated by men), ecological concerns and a sense of connectedness with all life forms on the planet, a reaction against ideologies and economic structures that widen the gap between rich and poor, the postmodern principle of uncertainty and rejection of any one "truth," the culture of technology, and an enlarged understanding of our power of knowing in transpersonal psychology.

Rather than be overwhelmed by the immensity of the task of reformulating a Christian philosophy of education that speaks to the hearts of people who are searching for connectedness and spiritual meaning, the time is right to pursue such an endeavor. The revolutionary leap in cultural consciousness will inform and shape a new paradigm of a Christian philosophy of education.

Christian teachers cannot make any particular claims in offering "value-centered" education. After all, there is no such thing as "valueless" education. However, the trend in western education to absolutize self has been detrimental to communal responsibilities. We cannot really appreciate self without community. Self is not autonomous. It is not the center of identity, nor is it a sole source of meaning. A Christian understanding of being embraces the wonder, mystery, suffering, and surprise of creation with its demands of stewardship. The basic orientation of Christian spirituality is union with God that flows into action for justice—as Jesus said, "Truly I tell you, just as you did it to one of the least of these who are members of my family, you did it to me" (Mt 25:40). Christ is both redeemer, to lead us to reconciliation, and reminder of who God is and who we might become. Christian education is holistic in that it seeks to lead students to a "fullness of life" as cooperative members of the earth community. Christian education is a carrier of the stories of the people. God's revelation in Jesus is a communication with the whole of creation (Col 1:15–17). It is a promise of hope at the marvel of God's merciful providence. Authentic Christian education is therefore infused with the spirit of optimism. A Christian philosophy of education provides a secure foundation for a teacher to follow a path of integrity.

Developing One's Integrity

How does a teacher develop a sense of integrity?

I propose the following ideas as stepping-stones to nurture the way of integrity:

- The active pursuit of the spiritual life, through prayer, readings, meditation, and works of justice.
- Formulating a personal mission statement and revisiting and revising such a statement at regular intervals.
- Evaluating the congruence between one's personal beliefs and actions.
- Becoming more aware of one's values and articulating these when appropriate.
- Being open to change and modification of one's values so that they are more aligned with gospel values.
- Working to become a person of trust and to esteem trustworthiness.

- Seeking the wisdom of mentors or spiritual directors.
- Incorporating helpful feedback into our character development.
- Growing in intimacy and love in significant relationships.
- Being accountable in communities.
- Savoring sabbath spaces for leisure and recreation.
- Engaging in action for justice.
- Learning from the accumulated wisdom of the heritage of human civilization.
- Keeping promises.

Teachers need to be proactive in fashioning a path of integrity. Working at the ideas stated above can motivate teachers to specify particular things they can do to translate ideas about integrity into practical behavior.

The enemies of integrity should be obvious from a reading of this chapter. I believe these foes to be duplicity, lack of personal awareness, inflexibility, arrogance, materialism, and individualism. The path of integrity assumes that a teacher will intentionally strive to attain this ideal of a truthful life. Bernard Lonergan, S.J., believes that a person's conversion to a worldview of integrity involves an intellectual, moral, and religious conversion. The fruits of this conversion are evident in teachers who move beyond a functional view of teaching and engage in teaching as an ethical enterprise.

Another way of illustrating the path of integrity is to suggest various images of a teacher. Each image suggests something about integrity.

Images of a Teacher
An image of a teacher is:

SHEPHERD
- leads sheep to lush pastures
- is courageous in the face of danger
- knows the sheep by name
- has a special love for lost ones
- is faithful to the flock

MYSTIC
- sees and makes connections
- knows the big picture
- draws things together in the unity of the Spirit
- is aware that everything and everyone is related

COMPANION
- enjoys fellowship
- celebrates and has fun
- stands in solidarity with others
- is a fellow traveler on the journey
- gives mutual support

ARTIST
- re-images our world
- stimulates the imagination
- relishes beauty
- evokes wonder
- celebrates sensuality
- delights in leisure
- recovers a fuller expression of humanity
- is subversive

JESTER
- suggests meaning—even in the absurd
- turns paradox into laughter

- names our humanity with its limits and potential
- keeps things in perspective
- exposes our foibles

SAGE
- discerns the way of integrity
- is a presence of Christ
- remembers the traditions
- tells the stories of the community
- listens to hearts
- is a prophetic presence

Which images of teacher appeal to you? Why do these images appeal to you?

Conclusion

We are not cogs in a mechanical world. We are created by God to enhance the quality of life in the earth community. Integrity leads us to teach from a perspective of values that reflect faith in God's creative energy through Christ. Integrity anchors our teaching on the inner truthfulness of discerned values. The way of integrity is like the hub of a great wheel. Its many spokes are teaching activities. The spokes of the wheel whirl about as teachers move through a diversity of tasks but the hub of integrity keeps the wheel of the teaching enterprise on a compass track of true north.

Reflection

To help you develop your own path of integrity, you may wish to work at the following activities:

1. Who has been (is) a significant person in the formation of your own values?

2. Identify two teachers who have had a positive influence on you.

3. What qualities did (do) you admire in these teachers?

4. What do you like about teaching?

5. What don't you like about teaching?

6. Why did you become a teacher?

7. Tell the story of your career as a teacher. Draw a graph to illustrate some of the highs and lows of your teaching career.

8. What are five key values for you as a teacher?

9. As a Christian what are three important religious beliefs that influence your values in teaching?

10. After reflecting on your responses to 1–9, draw together the values that you esteem as a teacher and compose your personal Teaching Credo Statement: "As a teacher I believe...."

If you belong to a school staff or the parish educational team, you may wish to share the individual Credos and compose a Mission Statement from the staff.

11. Meditate on these verses from Psalm 139:

You created my inmost self,
knit me together in my mother's womb.
For so many marvels I thank you;
a wonder am I, and all your works are wonders.

You knew me through and through,
my being held no secrets from you,
when I was being formed in secret,
textured in the depths of the earth.

2

WISDOM

The second essential quality for a teacher is wisdom. Recently a teacher recounted an incident in his classroom. His class was hosting a twelve-year-old boy from an African country who was competing in a school athletics carnival. The boy did not have any running shoes. The teacher took him to a sports store where he chose a pair of sneakers that were the most comfortable ones for running. When the teacher was telling the class about the shopping excursion, several of the students asked about the brand name and were stunned when the teacher said neither he nor the African boy knew or cared about purchasing the right brand name! Oh, the power of advertising!

Wisdom is the essence of the art of discerning what is authentic in living a life in accord with God's will and our human destiny. Wisdom presents a way of life that fulfills our aspirations toward wholeness. Wisdom is not only factual knowledge about something; wisdom implies judgment in the light of ultimate values. A Japanese proverb says: "Knowledge without wisdom is a load of books on the back of an ass." Each day teachers make many decisions about the best course of action toward particular students, how they teach lessons, whether to bring a simmering conflict with another staff member to a head, how to offer pastoral care to families with severe emotional needs. When we consider the various options facing teachers, we see how critical wisdom is. T.S. Eliot wrote these lines:

Where is the life we have lost in living?
Where is the wisdom we have lost in knowledge?
Where is the knowledge we have lost in information?
(*The Rock*)

What a challenge it is for teachers to help students come to a realization about life-giving values and expose the addictions in our society! Today electronic technologies are fashioning a new kind of consciousness and subtly manipulating communal attitudes and values. The concept of the global village is no figure of speech. The spectacular explosion of knowledge and information through the computer technology of the information superhighway and internet has heightened a global awareness of issues such as ecology, women's rights, peace, and the distribution of resources. Scientists have been interested in the phenomenon of how a relatively small group of people who acquire new behavior patterns can inform a large group of the population and create a new consciousness on particular social concerns. This phenomenon is known as "morphic resonance." It would seem that as low a percentage as one percent of the population can influence a new consciousness in society (O'Murchu, 11-12). However, morphic resonance is a two-edged sword. It is also fraught with danger when commercial corporations colonize society with materialistic values and images. The myth of consumer capitalism is promoted as the desired and dominant cultural story of the community. The danger is that the myth is posed uncritically and information is presented to us after it has been interpreted by social commentators. We can become passive recipients of daily doses of consumerism. Social commentators don't just report, they tell us their version of reality.

Enlightenment, seeing with a discerning eye, is one of the elements of wisdom. A Jewish story illustrates how we might learn to see with the eyes of the Spirit.

> An old rabbi asked his students how they might know that night was over and dawn had come. One student replied, "You know it is daylight when you see an animal in the distance and you can tell whether it is a sheep or a dog." "No," answered the rabbi. Another spoke up, "I think it is light when you look across the meadow to the trees and can distinguish a fig tree from the oak tree." "Not so," replied the rabbi. The students in frustration then called out, "Well how can you tell when night has ended and daylight has come?" The wise rabbi said, "It is when you look upon the face of any man or woman and see that person is your brother or sister. Because if you cannot do this, it is still night."

The gospel stories that record Jesus curing blind people stress that blindness is much more than a physical disability. In chapter 9 of John's gospel, the theme of blindness is elaborated with four groups of people, each group representing one position of faith or disbelief. The blind man who is cured eventually sees and acknowledges Jesus as "Lord"

(v. 38); the parents refuse to become involved (v. 21); the Pharisees become more obdurate in their blindness (v. 40); and the disciples struggle to make sense of the mystery of disability (v. 2). Through the gift of wisdom we come to see the real issues more clearly and move beyond the illusions that limit our understanding.

Biblical Understanding of Wisdom

Wisdom literature flourished in ancient Middle East cultures. The sage or wise person was regarded as a person who knew and communicated the principles of right living to the community. In early Greek culture, wisdom was seen as the attribute of those people who respected the gods.

The biblical figure of Wisdom—*Hokmah* (Hebrew), *Sophia* (Greek), *Sapientia* (Latin)—is the personification of God's presence in creation. Sophia is portrayed in diverse images in the Hebrew Scriptures. In the words of Dennis Edwards:

Wisdom's personification as a woman means far more than simply that the language used to speak of her is feminine. She appears, speaks and acts as a fully developed being, an attractive, mysterious, powerful and relational woman (Edwards, 20).

Wisdom:
- calls aloud in the streets (Prv 1:20);
- "is your life" (Prv 4:13);
- is the Creator's companion at the dawn of creation (Prv 8:30);
- is hostess to all who are "simple" (Prv 9:4);
- is the mother of all good things (Wis 7:12);
- represents the Torah, the Law (Sir 24:23);
- makes people into God's friends (Wis 7:27);

- is a reflection of the eternal light (Wis 7:26)
- leads and guides people on the path of light
(Prv 8:35);
- is beyond our comprehension (Jb 28).

The fear of the Lord is the beginning of wisdom (Prv 1:7). The wise person is contrasted with the fool who ignores the dictates of wisdom. If we accept the yoke of wisdom, we will receive immeasurable treasures (Sir 51:30).

Jesus the Wisdom Teacher

First-century Christians were drawn to portray Jesus as the Wisdom Teacher because this description seemed to encapsulate the special role of Jesus as teacher and symbol of personified wisdom. Paul speaks of Christ as "both the power of God and the wisdom of God" (1 Cor 1:24). Luke records the twelve-year-old Jesus listening and questioning the doctors of the Law in the temple. The temple teachers were "astounded at his intelligence and his replies" (Lk 2:47). The identification of Jesus as divine Wisdom is a theme in the writings of Paul and in the gospels of Matthew and John.

The most popular title for Jesus in the gospels is *didaskalos* or teacher. The title "teacher" is used forty-eight times in the gospels, and teaching *(didaskein)* is mentioned fifty times as the principal activity of Jesus. Greek cultural influence was very strong in first-century Palestine. In classical Greek culture there was a close bond of affinity and love between teacher and students. The mentor or teacher often lived with his students in a kind of community. As a teacher, Jesus followed this tradition. He gathered disciples to be his companions and empowered them to teach with powers of exorcism to authenticate their teaching (Mk 3:14–15). Together they traveled around the countryside, sharing a common purse (Jn 12:6), and preaching the Good News of the reign of God. The bond of friendship between teacher and the disciples was so intimate that the status of disciple was transformed to friend: "I call you friends because I have made known to you everything I have learned from my Father" (Jn 15:15). Jesus taught in a variety of settings. He taught in the synagogue (Lk 6:6–11), in the temple (Mk 11:17), by the seashore (Mk 4:1), and in the open countryside (Mk 5:1–12). He taught in Galilee, Samaria, and in Jerusalem. His teaching style was to tell stories or parables, to illustrate his teaching by healing and miracles, wisdom sayings, and symbolic actions. Above all, he gave authenticity to his teachings by the witness of his life.

The teaching career of Jesus did not last long, perhaps three years at the most before he was arrested and executed. Scripture scholars have analyzed the reactions to the teachings and ministry of Jesus. Most times there were no reported reactions. Over one hundred times, the gospels do not indicate any response at all. On at least thirty-nine occasions, there were positive reactions: "Everyone was filled with awe and glorified God saying: 'A great prophet has risen among us; God has visited his people'" (Lk 7:16). On nineteen instances, there were negative reactions to his teaching: "Then they began to implore Jesus to leave their neighborhood" (Mk 5:17).

The Theme of the Reign of God in the Teachings of Jesus

The reign or kingdom of God is the central message of Jesus' teaching. This theme appears over one hundred times in the gospels. Although there are many debates among scholars about its precise meaning, it would seem that Jesus was proclaiming a new world order which was to be characterized by right relationships founded on love, peace, and justice. What were the features of this world order as announced by Jesus? What are its implications for us as teachers? Let us examine key values of the reign of God as taught by Jesus the Wisdom Teacher.

Inclusion

God's grace is not restricted to a chosen few but embraces all who wish to respond positively to God's loving invitations, especially those who are marginalized by society. The model of table fellowship, as proposed by Jesus, includes all the unacceptable people—the prostitutes, the tax collectors, the sick, and the outcasts who were beyond the contempt of those who judged themselves holy and righteous before God and the Law. The stories of Zacchaeus (Lk 19:1–10), the woman at the well (Jn 4:1–42), the good Samaritan (Lk 10:29–37), and the father and the two sons (Lk 15:11–32) are examples of the startling message of inclusion. How do we as teachers cope with the less than perfect behavior of students? Who are the outsiders in our school and parish and in what ways are they included into mainstream school and parish life? Are people with disabilities fully integrated into the culture of the school and the parish community?

Priority

The quest for the reign of God must be one of urgency and must be given priority. The parables about the merchant selling everything to buy a pearl of great price and the story of the hidden treasure in the field (Mt 13:44–46) portray the imperative of ensuring that the kingdom is of utmost concern to us. For a follower of Jesus nothing takes precedence over the pursuit of implementing the reign of God. Do we as teachers concentrate on the important things with our students or do we tend to neglect major issues by getting lost in minor details of administration trivia?

Immediacy

The reign of God is not only an eschatological event (that is, it happens in the end). It is happening now. When the Pharisees asked Jesus when the kingdom of God was to come, he replied, "For look, the kingdom of God is among you" (Lk 17:21). The healing ministry of Jesus was a sign of the kingdom breaking through into world events. When the disciples of John the Baptist asked Jesus, "Are you the one who is to come?" (Mt 11:3), Jesus testified to his identity by pointing out his acts of mercy: "the blind see again, and the lame walk, those suffering from virulent skin diseases are cleansed, and the deaf hear ... and the good news is proclaimed to the poor" (Mt 11:4–5). Jesus is saying that the reign of God is announced not by empty rhetoric, but by what is already happening through healing and reconciliation. The reign of God does not simply happen only in churches or during religious education lessons, but is witnessed to and lived out in every interaction between teacher and student, however mundane these interactions are. We know the quality of a gospel value culture within the school and parish not by reading the school's mission statement, but by the experience of everyday school or parish life. How do we encounter Christ in rituals of hospitality? in the sports and cultural programs?

Hope

The parable of the mustard seed (Mk 4:30–32) reminds us that the reign of God does have a future. We will be surprised by the way God's power brings it into fruition in ways we could never imagine. How could a tiny mustard seed eventually produce branches large enough to allow birds to find shelter there? How could a wayward son who defied the laws of kinship be given authority by a prodigal father over the household (Lk 15:22)? The future does not depend solely on us. God is in control and will inaugurate the reign of God if we trust in God's loving providence. Are we hopeful teachers? Does our presence inspire students with a sense of optimism, even when their home or social environment looks bleak?

Solidarity

The reign of God announces a way of living whereby we live in right relationships and solidarity with each other. Jesus knew God as "Abba," a God of intimacy. The God "Abba" does not approve of barriers between people. The dualisms of black/white, rich/poor, male/female, first world/third world were utterly rejected by Jesus. Some feminist theologians suggest that we should use the word "kindom" rather than "kingdom" because "kindom" evokes images of family, kinship, and equity, while the word "kingdom" has a more patriarchal and hierarchical ring to it. How solidarity is actualized is described in the last judgment scene in Matthew's gospel (ch. 25). Entry to the kingdom is dependent on our solidarity with those in need of clothing, food, drink, shelter, and comfort. The poignant scene of Jesus dying between two thieves is a dramatic reminder of the example of Jesus to choose a place of solidarity with the outsiders of society. As teachers, are we comfortable with those who are not well educated or with those who are alienated or with those who are not of our cultural background?

The message of the reign of God provides a secure point of reference to critique the curriculum, culture, policies, and movements in education. Prayerful reflection on the values of the reign of God leads teachers to a stance of wisdom. Biblical studies show how the teachings of Jesus are in the tradition of wisdom literature. Early Christian writings refer to Jesus as "Sophia's prophet." The Beatitudes are a dynamic and particular expression of the teachings of Jesus as Wisdom Teacher.

The Beatitudes: A Wisdom Charter for Teachers

Just as every society posits a way of right living, the Beatitudes of Matthew's gospel set out eight features of wisdom living for followers of Jesus. According to Scripture scholar William Barclay, the Beatitudes "are not statements and prophecies of what is going to happen to the Christian in some other world; they are affirmations of the bliss into which Christians can enter even here and now" (Barclay, 11-12). The Greek word for "blessed" is *makarios*. It refers to the bliss that comes from living a life of goodness and thus sharing God's life. The "blessed" of the Beatitudes does not refer to a happiness emanating from the possession of material things but rather the inner peace that flows from a relationship with God in Christ. The Beatitudes provoke us to think about our sources of happiness. Many people live in quiet despair or imagine happiness as winning the lottery or being better off than anyone else. Have our religious symbols been subverted by the false image of the "good life"? Wisdom means following the teachings of Jesus.

Let us consider each of the eight Beatitudes as a charter for teachers who search for the path of wisdom.

How blessed are the poor in spirit;
the kingdom of heaven is theirs.

People who are poor in spirit depend on God's providential care. They discard the layers of ego needs and look to God for the transformation of their hearts. They inherit the kingdom because they possess the inner freedom to live by the values and vision of God's reign. They are prepared to renounce the constraints of self-centeredness. This self-surrender allows God's abundant grace to come to those who have accepted the in-dwelling of the Spirit. Meister Eckhart, a Dominican mystic of the thirteenth century, reminds us that the essence of spirituality is "subtraction," not "addition." The way of "subtraction" is to focus on the essence of our relationships with God, who is love. The way of "addition" is to become enmeshed in layers of protective icons that block God's initiatives. Teachers are poor in spirit when they are open to the giftedness of others and teach in a spirit of service. Poor in spirit people look to God for deliverance.

Blessed are the gentle;
they shall have the earth as inheritance.

The gentle people of this Beatitude are not insipid weaklings. On the contrary, they are so strengthened by the inner spirit that they have no need to oppress or manipulate others. The humility of gentleness is not about being a doormat but is the power of cooperative relationships. Humble people seek the will of God in trust. In return, God promises the fruitfulness of the earth. The earth has suffered from a failure of humankind to be gentle with her. A domination mode of relationships with earth has faded the colors of the covenant rainbow (Gn 9). The ravishing of the ecosystems jolts us into a realization about the need for gentle earth care. Gentleness heals and reconciles. A teacher is gentle when he or she allows students space and is respectful of their dignity. Gentle teaching may mean waiting patiently for the appropriate moment of learning.

Blessed are those who mourn;
they shall be comforted.

This wisdom saying is surely difficult to accept. How can we possibly find *makarios* or bliss in the trauma of sorrow? The fact remains that suffering or "mourning" is integral to human nature as it is in the dynamic evolution of all creation. In the letter to the Romans, Paul writes about the struggle between body and spirit (Rom 7:21–23). The tumult in creation, the grind and the glory of nature, is a sign of the cycle of creation, de-creation, and re-creation. Jesus never explained suffering but he lived it, especially through his passion and death. In some mysterious way, the descent into the pain of suffering is an ascent into the expanse of our humanity. Spiritual writers describe how the way of suffering is inseparable from the journey into wholeness. Psychologist Carl Jung believed that the way of individuation could not happen without incorporating the shadow. When we are thrown into the bottom of the well of pain, in faith we may discover God waiting there. Teachers who "mourn" have a capacity to share in the anguish of their students and members of the school community without being overwhelmed by it. In the gospels we read that Jesus wept on hearing of the death of his friend Lazarus (Jn 11:35). The Greek word *splagchnizesthai* is the strongest word for compassion. It conveys the meaning of being touched in the very depths of one's soul. Compassionate teachers listen to their own pain and share the comfort of healing through love.

Blessed are those who hunger and thirst for uprightness;
they shall have their fill.

First-century inhabitants of Palestine knew from bitter experience what it meant to be hungry and thirsty. The majority lived a precarious existence between having enough to eat and starvation. Although the wells and streams provided life-giving water for weary and thirsty travelers, they were not plentiful or always accessible. The craving for food is likened to the intense longing of a disciple for fidelity to the way of Christ. Being a follower of Jesus is not for the fainthearted. Discipleship demands a passionate longing for the realization of the reign of God. Teachers who "hunger and thirst for uprightness" have a keen sense of justice. They try to be just in all their dealings with their students and strive to be liberators when they perceive injustice in educational systems.

Blessed are the merciful;
they shall have mercy shown them.

Hesed or loving mercy is one of the central refrains of the Hebrew Scriptures. The story of God's merciful actions toward God's people is woven through the mission of the prophets, the covenant, the psalms, the exodus, and the heroes and heroines of Israel's history. A biblical understanding of mercy is not a negative thing, like a reluctant forgiveness after an event, but rather an outpouring of gracious love. Jesus epitomized the quality of love and mercy through his teachings and healing, especially in the supreme sacrifice of his life: "No one can have greater love than to lay down his life for his friends" (Jn 15:13). Teachers are reminded to be merciful as God is merciful to them.

Mercy is given without expectation of reward. Mercy is not a sign of weakness on the part of a teacher but an expression of unselfish love. Mercy releases us from the prison of hate.

Blessed are the pure of heart;
they shall see God.

People who see in the spiritual sense have the clarity of vision to discover God's presence in their world. The theme of "seeing" is a recurrent one in the great religions. The Greek word for "pure" is *katharos*, which suggests ritual purity. In this Beatitude, Jesus proclaims that we begin to see when we have interior purity. When we let go of the "riches" and addictions that block our relationships with God, then we really see. Teachers who strive to be "pure of heart" help students to clarify their values. They lead students to appreciate a moral code that affirms their dignity. To attain purity of heart, teachers need to nurture their own prayer life and acquire the habit of teasing out the values inherent in any course of action.

Blessed are the peacemakers;
they shall be recognized as children of God.

Early Christians refused to fight in the Roman army. They had inherited from Jesus a commitment to peace and reconciliation. This ideal of peace is hardly borne out, as the bitter divisions among various factions of Christians recounted in the the epistles attest. The Greek word for peace, *eirene*, suggests peace and harmony in relationships, rather than the cessation of war. This Beatitude does not praise those who merely speak about peace in school projects, but recognizes those who actually go out and make peace. Teachers are enjoined to be proactive in promoting multiculturalism, reconciling our native peoples, helping positive staff relations, and combating divisions. We admire Nelson Mandela, who helped forge peace in South Africa.

Peacemakers are courageous because they have to confront and overcome forces of violence and entrenched power. The starting point for peacemaking is peace within oneself. Teachers who are peacemakers assist the process of reconciliation and harmony within the community, the global village, and the earth.

> Blessed are those who are persecuted in the cause of uprightness;
> the kingdom of heaven is theirs.

The eighth Beatitude ends on a somber but realistic note. It sounds a warning about the price to be paid for being a witness to the ways of Jesus. Jesus bravely faced the consequences of his confrontation with the powerful religious establishment. Dietrich Bonhoeffer, a Lutheran pastor who denounced the Nazis, wrote about "costly grace" in his book *Letters and Papers from Prison*. He was hanged by the Nazis just before his prison camp was liberated by the allies. Sooner or later a faithful Christian is going to be challenged by forces that are threatened by the gospel message. Jesus warns us, "Be ready to pay a price for what you believe in." Teachers who raise awkward questions about unjust school policies or an expenditure on school equipment in preference to updating courses for teachers may find themselves quietly marginalized in the pecking order of who's who in the school.

The eight Beatitudes are a series of wisdom sayings which set the value tone of discipleship. They tell us how to attain *makarios*, the blessedness of sharing God's life. The Wisdom Teacher himself said, "I am the Way, the Truth, and the Life" (Jn 14:6).

Wisdom and the Cultural Environment

Teachers are eminently placed to help students evaluate cultural values from a wisdom perspective. We need to communicate and celebrate many good news stories about the generosity of people who unselfishly dedicate their lives to the service of others. Doomsday talk with youth can obscure the multitude of acts of commitment by students to the disabled, those with AIDS, the elderly, and famine relief projects. Wisdom teachers also expose the values inherent in the messages of our culture and critique them in the light of the gospel.

Our world is experiencing a dramatic shift in consciousness. Through networking and telecommunications technologies, we are beginning to think of ourselves as global citizens. Through the internet and the information superhighway, people with computers, faxes, and modems have direct access to political, social, and economic data as well as shared experiences which have an impact on their lives. Information is like a tidal wave. However, its very abundance challenges us to devise ways to assess its significance.

Another feature of our cultural consciousness is the emergence of meaning systems that are at variance with a religious cultural worldview. The philosopher David Tracy explains religious beliefs and behavior as a consequence of human beings seeking to interpret events beyond their control or comprehension. Traditionally, theistic religious systems have offered explanations of the mysteries of life, suffering, and destiny. The advent of a secular culture has spawned an array of "religions" that posit meaning systems for people who do not accept the interpretations of life presented by the churches. New Age ideas, the drug culture, sports, preoccupations with health, ecology, good life ideologies are examples of "religions" that attract many to their fold. A religious and artistic vision of society has been subverted by the dominance of an economic-technical paradigm of reality.

The mass media, especially television, is one such "religion" that has the power to shape our cultural images and tell our stories.

A U.S. study found that the 15-18 age group spent an average of 56.7 hours each week engaged in mass media consumption, with some groups watching up to 68 hours a week. In Australia, by the time a youth turns 18, she or he would have spent 20,000 hours—4 years—of waking time watching television. Studies show that the more one watches TV, the more one adopts the worldviews presented to the viewer. What are the beliefs presented by commercial television? Let us specify some common themes:

- Our self-worth is related to the possessions we have, the clothes we wear, the food we eat, the beverages we drink.
- We are more valued if we are Anglo-Saxon and male and belong to the middle or upper socioeconomic groups in society.
- The world is a violent place and we resolve differences by resorting to violence.
- Happiness is having a good time and owning lots of things.
- Relationships happen quickly and having sex is the expected thing to do.
- Complex issues can be easily resolved by simple solutions.

The cult of hedonism and individualism is promoted through the commercialism of the advertisers. The slogans of McDonald's ("We do it all for you"), or Coke ("Coke is it"), are designed to convey an impression of looking after all our life needs. In the Zakok papers, Horsfield describes how the ideology of consumerism proposes a view that our individual wants should be satisfied as a matter of priority. Never mind about our responsibilities of service to the community or sharing the joys and pain of people or working for justice! When the ideology of consumerism becomes a system, the gap widens between those in pursuit of luxuries and those who live in deprivation. The finite resources of the earth become dissipated in the production of goods that are extraneous to quality living (Horsfield, 8).

Reflections on the impact of mass media are not intended to denigrate its extraordinary contribution to the flow of information, entertainment, consciousness-raising in times of drought and ecological concerns, educational programs, and the democratic process of presenting different viewpoints on a whole series of contentious issues. However, for wisdom teachers, the issue of who tells the stories of the community is a critical one. Michael Warren, a prominent religious educator, writes,

> Stories are told with certain interests in mind. When parents tell children stories, it is because they want the children to understand certain matters they consider important or to entertain them by calling to their attention the fun or beauty or mystery of certain persons or events. When the story tellers and the stories change, what are the interests of the new story tellers and what lessons do their stories have? The agenda of the new nonparental, electronic story

tellers and their new stories are obvious to anyone who cares to watch television at the times children are expected to be watching. The basic interests are commercial, that is, toward selling (Warren, 371-372).

Television is a powerful influence in constructing images about our world and presenting norms for living.

The TV screen is a kind of picture window through which social commentators interpret daily events for us. The stories of our world are shaped by people who are unknown to us and governed by political and economic forces that often contradict the symbols and values of a religious culture. Electronic technology is a product of human ingenuity, and yet serious issues tend to be discussed superficially between commercials for toilet paper, cat food, and beer. TV commercials and print ads alike denigrate cultural icons— Aaron Copland's *Appalachian Spring* accompanies an automobile campaign, the Mona Lisa sells a correct breathing, anti-snoring device. What does this uncritical endorsement of western capitalism do to the power of the church to draw people to its own sacred story? The consumerist image of reality is a form of idolatry. Isaiah's invectives against idolatry have contemporary relevance, "The country is full of idols, they bow down before the work of their hands, before what their fingers have made" (Is 2:8). Wisdom teachers have the dilemma of combating a dominant consumerist myth while leading students to construct worldviews that touch into the deepest yearnings of the heart for happiness, love, and meaning. We need to teach the Christian story with enthusiasm and discover appropriate symbols to communicate the message. Teachers encourage students to question the prevailing myths of our culture and help them to dialogue between the Christ story and the strands of energy and concerns in society. Simply to denounce materialism and cultural stories, without offering an attractive alternative worldview, will reduce teachers to talking in an empty echo chamber. Teachers are well placed to assist students to forge links between a scientific and religious worldview and to bridge the schism between two realms of truth that appear to contradict each other's interpretation of reality.

One of the most difficult aspects of being a wisdom teacher is to hold fast to authentic values, such as priority of the person as opposed to excessive gain within the complexity of bureaucratic systems. Habermas, a contemporary German philosopher, describes a model of social reality with two distinct features. He uses the term "system" to designate that part of social reality that produces material goods and services. The other aspect of social reality is called the "lifeworld," the subjective world of values, dreams, communal stories, and myths. I would agree with Habermas's assessment that in consumerist oriented cultures, the "system" is "colonizing" the "lifeworld." A wisdom teacher who works in a bureaucracy will find it challenging to ensure that the system follows the lead of the values of the "lifeworld," and not the reverse.

How might wisdom teachers discover God's revelation and communicate to students a path for authentic living? The church's traditional way of seeking the will of God is the method of discernment.

Discernment

A time honored religious tradition of discovering God's will and wisdom is the shared model of discernment. The process of discernment is the faith stance of Christians that acknowledges that the Spirit is active when people gather in community. The promise of Jesus: "For where two or three meet in my name, I am there among them" (Mt 18:20) is a guarantee of the presence of Christ in the group. Teachers listen to the signs of the times and assist students to interpret their experiences in the light of the gospel. We read how Jesus became frustrated with the leaders for their inability or unwillingness to appreciate his message. He said to them, "When you see a cloud looming up in the west you say at once that rain is coming, and so it does. And when the wind is from the south you say it's going to be hot, and it is. Hypocrites! You know how to interpret the face of the earth and the sky. How is it you do not know how to interpret these times?" (Lk 12:54–56).

How does a teacher learn to be a discerning influence on his or her students? I suggest the following ideas for developing a wisdom style:

- Be a good listener; try to understand the various points of view expressed, especially when these views differ from your own.
- Accept that differences mean we have something to learn.
- Be well informed on topics through research and self-education.
- Pray for guidance of the Spirit.
- Take risks by becoming involved in experiences outside your routine circles so that your worldviews may be jolted into review.
- Nurture interpersonal relationships with family, friends, members of the school community, and other social groups.
- Savor and relish sabbath times to allow God's presence to transform your consciousness.

• Believe that no one person possesses all truth.

• Have healthy self-esteem and an honest knowledge of self and your personal motives.

• Learn to articulate ideas in a group and encourage feedback on these views.

• Develop a habit of weighing important matters prayerfully and being open to the consequences of various options if these ideas seem to be of the Spirit.

• Be humble.

• For more serious matters, allow time for decisions to be formulated.

• Believe that when we gather in the name of Jesus, he is really present.

These ideas may help you as a teacher to develop your quest for wisdom. The process of discernment leads teachers to ask questions of our cultural stories such as: "Who is esteemed?" "Who is left out of the stories?" "Would Jesus identify with the 'in' people of our cultural stories or the 'out' people? Why?" Good discernment is not a cop-out from a frank interchange of opinions. Nor is it an artificial attempt to wheel Jesus in on a wheelbarrow to solve a problem. It is a proactive process to affirm the quality of life under the guidance of the Spirit.

Conclusion

The path of wisdom encourages teachers to live by values which recognize their dignity and present an appealing religious vision of life. By supporting the many positive movements in our culture toward justice and equity, teachers support students in dismantling symbols of a false consciousness. The path of wisdom is to scrutinize those who tell the community's stories and to help oneself and others reimagine our stories according to the spirit of the dream of Jesus. Prudence is the governing virtue of the path of wisdom. Thomas Aquinas described prudence as that virtue which demands that we act cautiously and wisely. According to Aquinas, "Prudence is the reasoned regulation of conduct, reasoning well about the whole business of living well" (*Summa* 2-2, q.47, a.2).

Wisdom instructs us in how to live well.

The biblical view of wisdom portrays it as being present with God in the work of creation. The path of wisdom is an invitation to partnership in the wonder and energy of creation. Teachers who are wisdom people recognize the intrinsic value of all creatures and the responsibility to be faithful stewards within the earth community.

Reflection

1.Think about someone whom you consider to be a "wisdom" person. What qualities make this person a "wisdom" person?

2. Reflect on the growth of your own wisdom.

Who and what have been significant influences in your story of becoming a wisdom teacher?

3. Identify cultural forces which currently have an impact on your students. List the positive and negative forces.

As a teacher, how do you respond to these cultural forces?

4. Select three advertising commercials and three popular TV programs. Critique the values presented in the programs.

Which ones support a religious vision of life?

Which ones would conflict with the gospel message?

5. Compose your own definition of discernment.

Why is discernment so integral with the path of wisdom?

Focus on some aspect of school or parish life (e.g. pastoral care, learning process, enrollment policies, discipline, curriculum, decision making, communications).

Now set out a process using the discernment approach to examine one of these areas of school life and parish education programs.

6. Research the following Scripture passages about wisdom and then write a brief summary of a scriptural understanding of wisdom.

Prov 8:30	Sir 24:3–12	· Wis 7:25–26
Prov 9:13–18	Lk 11:31	Mt 12:42
Rom 11:33–34	Ps 103	Eph 3:10
Col 2:3		

3

GENERATIVITY

A s I write this chapter, memories and faces drift into my consciousness. I think of Betty, a religious sister in her mid sixties who taught English literature with the enthusiasm of a twenty-year-old. I can still visualize her demonstrating the drama of Shakespearean tragedies. I also remember Paul, who has long retreated into the fortress of his sterile teaching and counts the years and days until his retirement. As I think about Karen, a secondary teacher and single mother, I recall her sharing with me the stress associated with balancing the competing demands of her profession, her role as mother, and her role as caring daughter of very frail parents.

The teaching vocation is a calling to assist students in learning not only skills and curriculum content, but lasting and holistic life values. For this to happen, teachers need to be highly motivated people who enjoy teaching and feel that their enterprise is very worthwhile. Such a motivation is closely linked with the third quality of a very good teacher: generativity. Generativity is about choosing life and assisting students to live creatively through a realization of their potential.

What energizes you as a teacher? What are areas of stress for you? Teaching has its many personal rewards through the enjoyment of relationships with students and peers and facilitating learning. However, there are also debilitating forces which can lead to burnout and disillusionment. Teachers can and do experience stress from such forces as coping with constant change, being blamed by society for the "failures" of youth, disruptive student behavior, career path expectations, conservative resistance to parish sacrament programs, and personal feelings of inadequacy. A teacher may feel that he or she is walking on a treadmill of tasks that never end. How does a teacher attend to generativity? What does a teacher do to avoid stagnation or sterility? I propose a number of themes a teacher needs to address to enhance this important dimension.

Insight into the Life Journey

A teacher's first gift to students is the gift of self. Who we are speaks much more loudly than what we do or say. The quality of learning for students is significantly dependent on the quality of the teacher's working life. The power of a teacher's insightful and enriched life journey in the facilitation of learning cannot be underestimated.

A Jewish story tells of an absent-minded man who found it extremely difficult to locate his clothes when he got up in the morning. He became anxious before he went to bed at night because he dreaded not being able to find his clothes the next morning. One evening he decided to take things in hand by making a list of all his clothes and where he put them when he undressed. The next morning he was pleased with himself because, by following the list, he was able to find his clothes and get dressed. But when he was fully dressed, he asked in great consternation, "That's all very well to be dressed but where in the world am I?"

So we can be very organized, but not know who or where we are.

If we have insight into our own life journey, we may be better able to appreciate the passages and seasons of the ups and downs of our peers and students. The ebb and flow of the changing "seasons" of our winters, summers, springs, and autumns can leave us bewildered and feeling powerless to take control of what is happening. Insight into our life journey helps us make connections between the outer world of events and the inner core of our being, our spiritual center. We must attend to both journeys, the outer quest of identity and the journey of interiority. Jung writes of the urgency of linking number one person, the external face of our lives, with number two person, the interior source of being or Self. Jung's statement: "Do you want to go through life walking upright or dragged through by a series of events?" reminds us about the urgency of being proactive by integrating different events into a coherent worldview. If this integration does not happen, a teacher may experience a sense of being pulled in contrary directions by the incessant demands of family, students, parents, curriculum, system requirements, and personal agenda.

The practice of interiority allows teachers to move toward deeper levels of consciousness and interior freedom. Asceticism imposes healthy limits on our availability. Teachers are not always available or accessible to students or parents. They need their own sabbath spaces. A story from Jung's life illustrates this point.

Jung told one of his patients that he did not have time for

an appointment during the week. In the same week, the patient happened to be sailing on Lake Zurich and spotted Jung sitting on the wall of his home, dangling his feet in the water. At the next appointment, the patient angrily confronted Jung about his dishonesty in saying he was not available for an appointment. Jung replied, "No, I really did not have time to see you. You see, I had an appointment with myself and that appointment is one of the most important ones I ever have." Generativity can easily be stifled unless teachers preserve their quiet times which help them to align the energy of their tasks with their spiritual centers.

If teachers learn to tell their own stories, with all their mysteries, wonders, and paradoxes, they can become good listening companions to the unfolding life stories of students. The Aboriginal concept of *Dadirri* suggests an inner listening and attending to our own stories and the stories of those about us. To attend to one's life story is to become aware of how the Lord of the journey has led us through the times of light and darkness. The sense of incompleteness on the life journey is well expressed by a teacher friend of mine. Alana wrote, "When I started teaching, I thought I wouldn't survive; by the third year, I thought I knew it all. By my fifth year, I knew I was only beginning and would always have something to learn in order to be a good teacher."

Service

One of the paradoxes of generativity is that, for one to lead a fruitful life, one must shift the focus of psychic energy away from ego-self to service for others. This commitment to service is not a denial of true self but an expansion of our capacity to love and be compassionate. To adopt a stance of caring service is to discover life. Jesus said, "Anyone who finds his life will lose it; anyone who loses his life for my sake will find it" (Mt 10:39). The cross is a disturbing and puzzling symbol of generativity. Jesus did not back away from the terror of suffering but embraced his "hour" with courage. The washing of the feet is a poignant sign of the willingness of Jesus to set an example of *diakonia* or service (Jn 13).

The cult of individualism encourages us to find self-fulfillment through indulging every possible desire. Consumerist images portray illusions of happiness associated with the right skin cream, tropical island holidays, gambling at casinos, and driving the right car. The first Beatitude offers a different perspective on happiness: "How blessed are the poor in spirit" (Mt 5:3). Jesus warned his followers that the source of generativity is to be found in service: "Anyone who wants to be great among you must be your servant, and anyone who wants to be first among you must be slave to all. For the Son of Man himself came not to be served but to serve, and to give his life as a ransom for many" (Mk 10:44–45).

The work of teaching is certainly one of service. There are many long hours involved in successful teaching. Coaching, lesson preparation, pastoral care, staff and parent meetings, assessment, participation in the cultural life of the school, and gathering of resources are just some of the myriad of everyday activities that demand generous service. This attitude to service as taught by Jesus reflects an approach to power that is "servant power"—"power among us" rather than "power over us." Servant power is using our influence as teachers to liberate and create.

Being Proactive

Proactivity is the action we take in initiating responses according to our values instead of merely acting as a reaction to people and situations without reference to our beliefs. Proactive people assume control of their lives and reject any suggestion that we act according to how we have been taught to react. Proactive teachers lead students beyond the iron-bound assumptions of what is possible and help them think differently.

Reactive people allow others to set their life agenda. If teachers convince themselves that they are being swept along by rivers of bureaucracy, they experience a feeling of powerlessness. They become resentful and alienated because they perceive that there is no longer any freedom to subscribe to their own vision of teaching.

In Stephen Covey's language, their circle of influence contracts and their circle of concern is enlarged (Covey, 81-87). Reactive teachers tend to blame the government, the church, the media, society, and the curriculum for the problems they encounter. If teachers get into the habit of seeing the problem "out there," then that illusion reduces them to reactive behavior. Avoidance behavior does nothing but reinforce a sense of a teacher's personal impotence. Proactive teachers take positive steps to choose behavior that accords with their core values and they encourage students to imagine other possibilities of action.

Assertive behavior is a consequence of proactivity. Assertion is taking a middle course between being dominated by another's opinions and forcing our views upon others. Assertiveness is not about scoring victories or putting others down but is a choice for nonviolent interaction. Assertion flows from a healthy self-esteem and respect for the rights of people. Proactivity implies a new style of leadership that energizes a group to arrive at new solutions instead of being locked into a sterile culture of blame.

Love and Compassion

Love is the giving of something of self for the sake of others. Love is *the* energizing force of generativity. A loving teacher celebrates the gifts of relationships within circles of care. True love is received as well as given. There is no greater human need than to love and to be loved. So much of our worldview is derived from the ways in which we have been loved. Love is not confined to compartments of our being, it involves the whole person. The epistle of John summarizes the power of love, the heart of the Christian message, "My dear friends, let us love each other, since love is from God and everyone who loves is a child of God and knows God because God is love" (1 Jn 4:7–8). Teachers demonstrate their love by the little things—offering a cup of coffee to visitors, visiting a sick student or parent at home or in the hospital, sharing the joy of the birth of a child, saying hello to cafeteria workers, spending time with a staff member in need.

There are many limits to the way we love, especially the inhibitions that arise from fear and anxiety. In our quest for love, we become aware of its power and its fragility. We may fear that our love may not be reciprocated or it may be shattered by unresolved conflict. When we truly love, we become vulnerable to the ambivalences of relationships. Teachers need to send messages to their students that they too are emotionally vulnerable, but not too vulnerable. Otherwise, they will not cope with some of the bruising encounters that are part of teaching interactions. Students don't like teachers who are emotional robots. It is hoped that teachers will be nurtured by the love given and shared with family, friends, students, parents, and peers. Some of my best friends are past students, peers, and parents of students whom I have taught. Isolation and stagnation are enemies of generativity. Lortie's study of the work of school teachers indicates that isolationism is well established in the culture of teaching (Lortie, 1975). Another foe of generativity is the expectation that the children or adults we teach will satisfy our emotional needs for love.

Loneliness is the paradox face of love. Teachers are surrounded each day by people but they can be very lonely. Loneliness is an inescapable human condition which Augustine describes in his famous statement, "Our hearts are restless, Lord, and they will not rest until they rest in thee." Teachers may cope with feelings of loneliness by becoming submerged in overscheduled activities or they may withdraw into a detached isolation. Both responses are flawed and negate opportunities to grow into love. Why not take the risk of believing that we are lovable and loved unconditionally by God? St. Catherine of Siena (1347-1380) wrote, "Nails would not have fixed Christ to the cross unless love had held him there."

Compassion is the "weeping with" those in need. Jesus enjoins us "Be compassionate just as your Father is compassionate" (Lk 6:36). Compassion means being in solidarity with the basic human sameness in every person. Teachers show their compassion by companionship with those who suffer and by supportive action. Compassion involves moving from a point of detached and clinical observation to becoming involved with all the related inconvenience. Compassionate teachers do not retreat to the safety net of their teacher status. They take time to listen to students, arrange for special services, visit the hospital, recognize multicultural differences, be friends to the lonely.

Care of Self
The strength of generativity is closely related to the value

we place on ourselves. Those who denigrate themselves and engage in self-flagellation deny part of their humanity. When we befriend our whole self, including our foibles, we discard the "halo" illusions of self. A healthy self-regard is not overly disturbed by criticism. A positive self-image protects us from seeking approval from students and peers in ways that compromise our integrity. Neither do we apologize for our existence. When we ignore excessive ego needs we are freed to give willing service.

Care for self is neither self-indulgence nor complacency. Care for self might imply learning to say a big NO to extra work. It may insist on more rest and leisure; it reins in haphazard approaches to addressing tasks. We are gradually coming to an awareness of the need to heal those aspects of the church story which split body and soul. The influence of Neoplatonic thinking in early Christianity tended to dilute the power of the doctrine of the Incarnation and the essential oneness of the human person. God's identification with the human condition was an affirmation of the celebration of the unity of body and soul. The body is the physical manifestation of the spirit or soul of a person. It is not separate from the soul. Care of self suggests that teachers are attentive to health matters through dieting, exercise, and abstention from addictive practices, such as excessive alcohol consumption, which diminish health.

Care for self implies a wholesome sexuality and acknowledgment of our female and male identities. The celebration of being male and female expresses the gift of relationships and partnership, the mystery and power of sensuality, and the integration of self and body (Whitehead, 46). A useful question to consider is, "As a woman (or as a man), what do I most enjoy about my sexuality? What do I find most constraining about my sexual identity?"

We also care for self by attending to the harmonizing of our feelings and reason. Our emotions are guides to the direction of our passions. Holistic living embraces both head and heart and empowers us to use our emotions intelligently (Goleman, 29).

Fun

Fun and humor enliven the path of generativity by putting things into perspective. Laughter turns solemnity on its head. The staff jester is surely destined for glory although, as a teacher, I may be more reticent about endorsing the student jester's role, especially during my carefully prepared lesson! Humor exposes the absurdities of life. Fun in sport, family games and outings, dance and entertainment allow a welcome release of energy. After a stressful day, I find great delight in playing with Sammy, our border collie dog, who lives for play (and chewing bones). As I get out of the car Sammy comes bounding up, drops the tennis ball at my feet, and pleads with me to throw the ball for a game of catch. One of my favorite passages from Scripture is the creation scene as described in the book of Proverbs where wisdom is at play with the Creator:

> I was beside the master craftsman,
> delighting him day after day,
> ever at play in his presence,
> at play everywhere on his earth,
> delighting to be with the human race (Prv 8:30–31).

Fun breaks the soul-destroying cycle of the tyranny of an overscheduled existence. Fun and creativity are close allies. Some years ago when I felt creativity was drying up within me I penned these lines:

Now I take my lamp
To find my inner lost child.
Stay with me holy child.

As a teacher, what do you do to nourish your creativity
and imagination? The path of generativity is enriched by joy
and laughter (Jn 15:11). Do you have a sense of personal
adventure in life? Why not undertake a new project each
year? Are you a risk taker?

Community

The New Testament presents community living as a radical ideal of *koinonia*, of people loving one another in a new
style of relationship, not according to kinship or status but
as sisters and brothers in Christ (Jn 15:12; 1 Jn 3:11; 2 Jn 1:5).
Teachers belong to a number of communities. Apart from
the school community, they may be members of a parish,
Lions Club, or other social and family groups. Generativity
is supported and developed by belonging to a caring community.

By nature, human beings tend to gather together to share
values, participate in supporting networks of relationships,
and respond collectively to mutual concerns. The word
"community" is a difficult word to define because it is
understood so differently according to a wide spectrum of
expectations about what a community is intended to be.
Some teachers, for example, may be satisfied with their
school as community if the school provides a sound education for students without any expectation of personal emotional investment in the social group. Other teachers would
anticipate that members of the school community would
develop close emotional bonds and be supportive of one
another. Communities are complex social groups with many

levels of participation and motivations for membership.

What are key features of a genuine Christian community? Although there is no such a thing as an ideal community, it may be helpful to specify certain features of community that offer a reference point in evaluating the authenticity of a learning Christian community. Consider these, which I have gleaned from my experiences of working with various community groups:

- People in the group share a common vision and task.
- The culture of the group is oriented toward both task and people.
- There is an agreed purpose among group members.
- An accepted process for decision making ensures significant participation by its members.
- People care about one another.
- Good communications facilitate relationships.
- The work of teaching and learning is a priority.
- Leadership empowers members to achieve their work by utilizing the gifts of the people.
- There is a commitment among members of the group to build community.
- People celebrate and ritualize special times in the life of the community.
- Members pray regularly.
- New members are welcomed.
- Differences and diversity are seen as opportunities to grow as a group.
- Ongoing development at a personal and professional level is encouraged and facilitated.
- There is a network of pastoral care.
- Effective interactions occur between the communi-

ty and other social groups in the wider community. People have to balance the demands of a series of interacting social groups.

• The structures of the community are organized so as to ensure an effective utilization of resources.

• Group members are open to change.

The features of community mentioned above provide you with a framework for reviewing your own learning community. Which features are strengths of your community? Which ones need to be developed? Is your learning community a support for your way of generativity? On many occasions, I have been touched by the stories of teachers who attributed their psychological survival in times of extreme personal crisis to the loving support of their school communities. Sustaining the vital life of a learning community challenges a teacher to evaluate her or his own investment in its dynamics. Good communities do not happen by chance. We have to work hard to attain an effective community and to maintain its vitality. How important is community for you?

According to Mark's gospel, Jesus devoted much of his public ministry to forming the disciples in the ideals of *koinonia* or a way of partnership in community. The ideals of early Christian communities offered a stunning new vision of how people might live cooperatively, sharing their possessions (Acts 4:32). This radical life-style was in sharp contrast to the prevailing culture of status and privilege as determining the identity of a person in a social group.

Healing and Reconciliation

Generativity can be perverted by alienation and unresolved hurts. If hurts are not healed, they begin to fester and absorb our psychic energies into feelings of anger and revenge. Because it is an interactional work, teaching is certain to cause hurts as well as generate love and positive feelings. We all need to face the demons of anger and hurt. Unforgiveness can hold us in a vise-like grip and cripple our capacity to love. Forgiveness liberates. Holding grudges against students or other staff members blocks any kind of meaningful relationship. Teachers learn to forgive and ask for forgiveness. Asking forgiveness is both humbling and freeing. Envy and jealousy are twin forces of evil that stunt reconciliation.

The following suggestions for healing hurts may be helpful for teachers:

• The hurt must be acknowledged and faced.
• It may be useful to articulate the hurt with a sympathetic but challenging friend or mentor.
• One must be prepared to let go of the hurt and move beyond it.
• Pray for healing; allow time to pass to give some perspective to the hurt in the broader sweep of one's life journey.
• Find support with caring people.
• Affirm one's self-worth.
• Be proactive in opening other possibilities in relationships rather than being trapped in an acid pot of unresolved hurts.

Healing is also facilitated between diverse cultural groups. Teachers can do much to bring together multicultural groups and break down the barriers of ethnic stereotypes.

Spirituality
Spirituality is a relatively recent word in the history of the

church. The word began to be used at the beginning of the seventeenth century in French religious circles. However, the quest to discover a transcendent meaning to the questions of life and death has always been characteristic of the way humankind has reacted to the mystery of existence. Spirituality is our response to the big questions of life and death. Christian spirituality expresses our relationships with God in Christ through the power of the Spirit. Christian spirituality involves one in an active pursuit of justice.

In faith we believe that we are created in the image of God and, therefore, are spiritual beings by our very nature. Our sexuality and generativity reflect the divine fecundity or life source of God the Creator. Vatican II reminded us that the call to holiness is for everyone, not just a chosen few. A teacher's spirituality is nurtured by prayer, meditation, works for justice, and participation in sacramental life, especially the eucharist. But above all, spirituality is experienced through the daily living of the gospel message in family relationships, mundane teaching tasks, and allowing ordinary things to be graced. Our point of reality is our moment of grace. Our students have much to teach us about spirituality. Sharing their highs and lows, rejoicing at that flash of insight, participating in candlelight vigils or campaigns for a just cause are examples where we may encounter God through our students. And those quiet moments in the home or garden, or walking or listening to music, are times to savor the Lord's presence. In the words of the poet Noel Davis, "O how alluring You are in the soft light of silence." A teacher's enthusiasm for spirituality springs from her or his passion for spreading the Good News.

Christian spirituality is Trinitarian in its essence. The Trinity is the core metaphor for God's nature. When we speak of God as Trinity, we explore the profound mystery of God's generative life which participates and energizes all of creation. God is source of life (Father); God is witness to compassionate love (Son), God is nurturer of life and bond of love (Spirit). The Trinity is not an intellectual concept of a triangle or a mathematical impossibility but a feeling, passionate God who laughs and cries with creation. The metaphor of Trinity speaks about a God whose very nature is sexual, communal, and generative. Because we are made in the image of God, we are trinity people—sexual, communal, and generative. The Trinity of God is a beautiful symbol of the interdependence of all things in creation and the organic nature of the universe.

Pastoral Care

A teacher's role in helping students to be creative learners is implemented through sound teaching within a context of pastoral care. The term "pastoral care" refers to the exercise of care by teachers, students, parents, and administration in the integration of the academic, religious, and social dimensions of school life. The scope of pastoral care includes the whole of the curriculum and the school community. How teachers approach pastoral care is an indicator of how they perceive their role as teachers.

If teachers appreciate their work as a vocation to promote the generativity of their students, then their teaching horizons extend much wider than curriculum content. They share something of the mystery and excitement of sharing the dreams and possibilities of the students whom they teach. Good pastoral care teachers maximize every opportunity to impart values of mutual respect and cooperative living. They have a special concern for drop-outs from the school system and the socially alienated. If having a purpose with substance is one of the key elements of generativity, then being an effective pastoral care teacher is an impelling motivation for a sense of mission in one's life.

Responding to Stress

Statistics about the growing number of stress-related worker's compensation claims confirm that teachers work in one of the most stress-related careers. Teacher stress is the way in which teachers respond to the demands of their job. The word "stress" is often used in a negative way. However, nothing would change without some kind of stress. The stress referred to in the statistical data is "dystress" or dysfunctional stress which is detrimental to health and emotional stability. For a teacher, the causes of stress may be associated with the inability to cope with obstinate and violent students, curriculum demands, work overload, feelings of personal inadequacy, dysfunctional relationships, and system-induced factors such as professional requirements. A significant factor in stress is actually not the problem itself but the attitude to the problem. One teacher can be excited about change in the curriculum as an opportunity to develop new teaching approaches; another teacher may be thrown into a high state of anxiety about the perceived inability to cope with the curriculum change. Interior "self-talk" conversations such as, "What if I fail?" or "Will I be able to cope?" can induce anxiety. Our bodies are punished by stress which generates feelings of exhaustion and makes us more prone to catch every passing germ.

Teachers need to face up to the prospect of being victims of dysfunctional stress and take positive steps to safeguard their life of generativity by affirmative coping actions. The ideas presented below are a brief summary of helpful ideas about responding to the pressures of teaching:

• Monitor the interior voices, especially the anxious voices which raise all kinds of forbidding things that may happen. Test out these fears and exaggerations against the reality of evidence from past happenings. Imagine a worst case scenario, then check out the expectations you place on yourself. You may have to rescript your interior programs of self-talk. Sometimes problems can be your friends.

• Learn to relax mentally and physically. If you feel bad about something, relax mentally and monitor the feelings. Get in touch with the feelings and find out what is causing them. Look for ways to respond more creatively to the causes. Practice deep breathing or simple relaxation exercises such as unlocking knees, stretching fingers, walking outside, plucking and rubbing a leaf.

• Pray for strength and guidance. Meditation is a calming and centering influence. Repeat a mantra slowly (e.g., "Come Holy Spirit, fill the hearts of your faithful").

• Discuss your stressful situation with a wise friend.

• Become proactive in planning ahead so as to anticipate problems wherever possible. Develop strategies to respond to these problems long before they appear. Learn ways of being assertive so that other people or events do not set their agendas for you.

• Have plenty of fun times so that pent-up energy finds a healthy release. Family and friends can be a source of restoration.

• Develop skills in communications, conflict management, planning, and time scheduling so that you have confidence in handling stressful interpersonal relationships.

• Accept the limits of what you can reasonably do and what you simply can't achieve. Find a balance between complacency and personal challenges to do better.

• Laugh at yourself and others. Thomas Merton wrote that humor is an invitation "to cast our awful solemnity to the wind and join in the general dance."

• Acknowledge that others can help you through difficult times. Don't be afraid to ask for help and say, "I need you."

• Set realistic goals and regularly check to see how these goals are being accomplished. Establish priorities of what you must accomplish.

• Know yourself well enough to recognize the danger signals that are warning you to slow down.

• Keep things in perspective. There is an ancient saying, "The mountain shamed the molehill, until they both were humbled by the stars." Another saying I cherish is, "The wise person points to the moon, the fool studies his fingers."

A teacher's generativity can be stifled by stressful situations that are not creatively addressed. If stressful events are handled wisely, they can generate new energy for the achievement of the tasks.

Partnership with Earth

The universe is an integral community, that is, every single particle is somehow related to the intricate network of relationships in creation. Francis Thompson wrote in *The Mistress of Vision:*

All things by immortal power

Near or far ...
To each other linked are,
That thou canst not stir a flower
Without troubling a star.

A paradox in our universe is that although everything is differentiated into categories, everything is also one in totality. It is difficult to celebrate the generativity of humankind apart from the fecundity of the earth community and the Creator. A teacher's generativity leads him or her into a communion with the earth. The mutuality of relationships does not stop with humankind but extends to all creation. As stewards of creation, we reverence the plurality of all life forms and exercise care for their well-being. A teacher's love of the earth is infectious with students. Teaching earth care ethics is one aspect of this attitude of awe. Caring for the environment through tree planting, clean-up campaigns, forest walks, preservation of species, and a creation-centered curriculum are other avenues for a teacher to convey something of the wonder and mystery of God's earth. One of my special delights is cultivating a rainforest on our property. Each tree is one more tiny contribution to the health of our mother earth. Our decision to choose life cannot be separated from a commitment to participate in caring for the planet.

Purpose in Life

To discover meaning is a fundamental motivation for the pursuit of life. A friend of mine is always exhorting my circle of friends to find our passions, see if they are worthy enterprises, and then follow their directions. If teachers prize their profession as a vocation to do something good for the community, then they will have that deep satisfaction of knowing their life work is fruitful. Without an exalted purpose, teaching becomes nothing more than a mechanistic interchange of information rewarded by monetary payment. The celebration of a meaningful life leads one to a sense of blessing or *berakah*. Instead of worrying about all the things we are not or have not, we rejoice in the giftedness of every expression of life itself.

Conclusion

Generativity is a quality that celebrates life in its diversity and possibilities. The profession of teaching with its responsibility for the education of others is fraught with pitfalls related to stress and overscheduling. To motivate students to choose positive ways of living, teachers themselves need to care for self and treasure their gift of generativity.

Reflection

1. Make a list of all the things that energize you in teaching.

2. Specify the things that limit your generativity or feeling of being alive.

3. From your observations as a teacher, which aspects of teaching help teachers to be generative people? Which contribute to burnout or excessive fatigue?

4. Consider how your school situation or teaching environment might be improved to enhance the quality of life and support for members of the school community or the parish education team.

5. Reflect on the various themes in this chapter about a life of generativity. Which theme is most relevant to you now? Why?

6. Who is (was) the most "alive" teacher you know (knew)?

What are (were) the characteristics which make (made) this teacher "alive"?

7. Compose a personal plan to nurture your generativity during the next six months. When you have drawn up your plan, discuss it with another member of the staff or a friend.

8. Compose a motto for generativity.

4

LEARNING

A friend was recounting the story of his daughters at school. The elder daughter loved her teacher and her learning went ahead in leaps and bounds. Next year, the parents were thrilled when their younger daughter was assigned to the same class. They rejoiced to know that their younger daughter would likewise profit under the guidance of such a competent and caring teacher. Imagine their surprise when their younger daughter arrived home in floods of tears, threatening to do school by correspondence if she had to endure another day with such a horrid creature as her teacher. No amount of daughter-parent-teacher dialogue could change the dynamic of alienation. Ah, the mystery of learning!

Teaching is about the facilitation of learning and the liberation of hearts and minds through learning. This fourth quality reflects on how people learn and what helps them to learn. It sets the learning process within a philosophy that is aligned with a Christian vision of education. Who can be a teacher without first being a learner? When we consider the various contexts of learning we realize the diversity of our learning experiences. We learn from our family, the social environment, schooling, the vagaries of our life journeys, the local and world community, and our religious faith. Teachers have traditionally been regarded as *loco parentis*, or acting for parents.

Technology and Learning

A recent newspaper survey estimated that seventy percent of our students who leave school in ten years time will take jobs that do not now exist, using technology that has not yet been invented. In our contemporary world, technologies for learning are assuming a central place in the learning process. New communications technology, such as the internet, provides extensive information to businesses, homes, and schools. The internet gives access to, and personal control of, information. Students can now communicate through computers with teachers in other towns and countries. However, there are many issues about the technology of the information superhighway that are unresolved. Some of these concerns are the growing gap between schools that are financially able to afford this technology and those that cannot; the plight of teachers—surveys reveal that only about twenty to thirty percent of teachers are computer literate; the difficulty of changing school approaches to learning modes and styles; a process for sifting through the flood of information; the potential decline in communal learning when so much information can be accessed through personal computers. What is clear is that teachers must become much more proactive in shaping the appropriate utilization of the internet, otherwise, the information superhighway system will speed off at its own pace leaving behind confusion about the nature of learning and its impact on the schools. A basic question, too, is which theories and practices of learning are congruent with a Christian philosophy of education. Let us now pose a number of questions intended to clarify a teacher's beliefs about learning.

Questions about Learning

We know that ultimately learning lies with the students. They learn what they choose to learn. However, teachers need to think about the process of learning they facilitate. The following questions may help you clarify your own beliefs about approaches to teaching and learning:

- Am I always looking for ways to improve my approaches to learning?
- Am I aware of my preferred teaching and learning style?
- Do I structure learning experiences to suit the varied preferred learning styles of my students?
- Which of my current practices of teaching can I let go to make room for new approaches to learning?
- Are my practices of learning and teaching congruent with my beliefs and values?
- How are my Christian values reflected in my teaching structures and practices?
- To what extent do I understand the world of my students in order that I choose the most appropriate learning styles for them?
- What new learning styles have I developed with or for my students in the last three years of teaching?
- How often do I evaluate the effectiveness of the process for learning that I use in my teaching?

• What learning experiences most energize me?

• Do the learning approaches I employ lead my students to creative citizenship or do they merely impart content to the students?

• Are the rewards for learning for both students and teachers appropriate?

You might like to spend some time in pondering these questions and identifying the questions that affirm, challenge, or disturb you.

You may also find it helpful to clarify your own beliefs about students by responding to the following statements with a "yes" or "no" or "not sure" in the appropriate column. These provocative statements are intended to help you appreciate the range of views on the continuum of learning.

Statements	Yes	No	Not sure
1. Students are so different in learning abilities that all the teacher can do is teach the curriculum.			
2. Students need to learn about the process of analysis as well as arriving at the right answer.			
3. The amount of content to be covered leaves little time for student discussion.			
4. Teachers need to role model behavior in order to develop a thoughtful classroom.			
5. Getting the correct answer is the desired result in learning.			
6. Education is the acquisition of specifically defined bodies of knowledge.			
7. Content is changing so rapidly that processes for learning are what must be taught.			
8. The focus of activity should be on the students not the teacher.			
9. The students' task is to know the best answer to each problem.			
10. The goal of learning is to create self-directed, thoughtful students.			
11. Some students pass, some students fail.			
12. Content is valuable for its own sake.			

Your responses to these questions may help you to appreciate your own stance on learning. Spend some time thinking about the statements that are congruent with your own philosophy of learning and those that conflict with your beliefs on learning.

It is helpful for teachers to explicate their philosophies of learning and to evaluate their classroom practices in light of the values they hold about learning. School and classroom structures, inadequate parish facilities, a lack of resources and professional support, entrenched traditional models of teaching in the school culture—all these can be formidable obstacles to teachers who wish to modify their own approaches to the learning process.

One aspect of learning is the perceived relevance of content by students. A common student criticism of content is that it is pointless. Students may judge that much of the content of their curriculum leads them nowhere and is irrelevant. Recently I read about a religious sister who was interviewing a parent about her son's school record and the issue of his poor spelling came up. Sister Frances said to the mother, "Paul even failed to spell 'Egypt' correctly the other day." The mother retorted, "Well, what of it? You can spell 'Egypt.' I can't spell 'Egypt' either, but I've got eight kids and you don't have none!" Another story illustrates the same theme. A philosopher was being ferried across a river by a boatman. The philosopher said to the boatman, "Do you know about philosophy?" "No," answered the boatman. "Then," said the philosopher, "you have lost one third of your life." The philosopher asked further, "Do you know any literature?" "No," said the boatman, "I don't know any literature." "Then," replied the philosopher, "you have lost two thirds of your life." Just then the boat struck a rock and began to sink rapidly. The boatman asked the philosopher, "Do you know how to swim?" "No," cried the philosopher. "Well, sir," said the boatman, "you have lost your whole life!"

Teacher as Facilitator of Learning

During the 1960s and the 1970s there was considerable ferment in educational circles about school and classroom practices. I recall two books in particular that had a great impact on me in provoking me to think more carefully about my classroom practices. J. Holt's *How Children Fail* and I. Illich's *Deschooling Society* represented the genre of literature in the progressive movement that asked searching questions about the relevance of the curriculum and the structures of schools as places of learning. The emergence of alternative schools (e.g. Summerhill in England) challenged the more traditional schools to evaluate their assumptions about learning and classroom practices. Richard White, in his article *Questionable Assumptions Underlying Secondary School Classrooms* (311-330), specified fifteen assumptions that inhibit good education. Although these assumptions refer to secondary schools and recent innovative educational practices have discarded some of them, I believe that they are still relevant points for discussion in many schools, even in some elementary schools. Here is a summary of these assumptions:

- Schools must be divided horizontally, i.e., learning is conducted in grades or year groups.
- School years are a natural division of time that must be observed in all curriculum arrangements.
- School subjects are taught in specific periods.
- Learning is competitive, not cooperative.
- Teachers rule the classroom.
- Teachers must reward and punish.
- There are good teachers and bad teachers and that is a given for how schools are.
- To learn is to acquire knowledge. To teach is to cover content.
- Readiness for learning is defined by age and grade, not by a student's readiness.

• Everyone in the class should learn the same content.
• Students and learners are not responsible for what is
to be taught. The content of the curriculum is set by
outsiders.

Teachers may well consider if these assumptions are
valid by looking at how learning is conducted in their
school. A traditional teaching style leads to four assumptions. Students learn best when they are:

• isolated—in rows and separate from others;
• silent—discussion is not good for learning;
• away from friends—split up peer groups;
• in age groups—no multi-age interaction.

As a teacher you might like to reflect on the above observations about the more traditional assumptions about learning in school. Consider if vestiges of these assumptions
remain in your school. You may also have to deal with your
own frustrations when financial, political, or other factors in
your school limit your aspirations to improve learning practices. Often we have to compromise between the ideals and
the reality imposed by finance and curriculum.

Let us now suggest ways to enhance learning.

Facilitating Learning

How does a teacher facilitate learning? Here are a number of ways to consider:

1. If a teacher acts in the role of companion learner, then
students may come to appreciate learning as an ongoing
process, a useful thing to do. A teacher is not simply a dis-
penser of information but one who is enthusiastic about

opening new windows of knowledge and experience.

2. Every effort is to be made to create thoughtful learning stations where students are taught to engage in complex-level thinking. Robert Hutchins writes, "My idea of education is to unsettle the minds of the young, and to inflame their intellects." A thoughtful learning station is not one where occasional problems are posed for discussion but where teachers and students are involved in thoughtful discourse on a regular basis (Udall & Daniels, 2).

3. A climate of respectful listening will support reflective teaching and learning. Teachers and students come to appreciate the inner listening of attending—not only to the words spoken, but to the body language and the emotions expressed. Students and teachers cannot engage in complex thinking unless there is a commitment to attend thoughtfully to what is being communicated.

4. Students are encouraged to question, probe, evaluate, and disagree with one another. Teachers will help students break with the tyranny of getting the right answer so that they are prepared to take risks in searching out optional responses to questions.

5. Learning is not restricted to verbal interchanges. It happens also through hands-on activities, music, dance, poetry, silence, drama, and personal project work. Learning through creative silence allows the outer and inner learnings to be connected in a new totality. Such learning moves us away from being trapped by the limits of head learning. Play is a useful ingredient of learning where students learn in an environment free from structural boundaries.

6. A positive learning culture creates mistake zones where teachers and students can make mistakes without the stigma of failure. If something is not understood, then people need to feel free to say so without being regarded as stu-

pid. Constructive feedback, if received, leads to improved learning.

7. There must be sensitivity to any gender bias in learning and an honoring of different multicultural styles and traditions in learning. Learning styles are adapted to people with special needs and (dis)abilities.

8. Cooperative learning emphasizes the communal power of learning and social skills involved in learning together rather than individualistic learning in a competitive mode. Math classes, for example, can be transformed by cooperative peer tutoring.

9. Teachers need reassurance that the development of cooperative learning methods does not mean the threat of abandoning teaching strategies that have worked for them in the past. Cooperative learning may in fact add to their store of wisdom.

10. Rapid advances in communications technology provide exciting opportunities to learn in radically different ways from traditional classroom methods.

11. Teachers and students need to understand the different kinds of thinking illustrated by De Bono's "Six Thinking Hats" (De Bono, 31-33). In De Bono's schema, the six hats are:

White hat: An objective look at data and information
Red hat: Feelings, hunches, and intuition
Black hat: Logical negative, caution, judgment
Yellow hat: Logical positive, feasibility, benefits
Green hat: New ideas and creative thinking
Blue hat: Control of the thinking process

Although these images may be questioned by other learning theories, teachers can assist students to appreciate the diversity of thinking by putting on a hat of a particular color and having students think in that particular mode.

12. The scope of learning embraces emotional learning, or emotional literacy, whereby people are assisted in harmonizing the activities of the emotional brain and the thinking brain (Goleman).

13. Within the framework of the Myers-Briggs indicators, teachers and students come to recognize that their thinking is influenced by their psychological types (e.g., a sensate will prize useful and practical learning; the intuitive will see connections and engage in flights of imagination; the person with a dominant thinking function will enjoy intellectual explorations; while the feeling type will delight in the social relationships of the learning experience). This framework does not put people into stereotyped learning boxes but helps teachers become more aware of the influence of psychological types on thinking and learning modes.

14. Research into the different ways in which right and left hemispheres of the brain process information reveal that the left brain is more linear and sequential while the right brain is more creative and simultaneous. Learning activities need to take the two modalities into account in order for holistic learning to occur.

15. Until recently, the majority of literature and research on learning was produced by men. The emergence of feminist writers and researchers reminds us that we need to draw on the insights of both women and men if we are to appreciate the nature of learning.

16. Learning should happen with a minimum of coercion. William Glasser in his book *The Quality School—Managing Students without Coercion* portrays the "boss-manager" type of school which operates out of a model of control and imposed discipline. Learning is regulated and mandated

within clearly defined parameters. Glasser contrasts the "boss-manager" school with the "lead-manager" school which works out of a culture of persuasion and cooperation. Learning is encouraged as a cooperative venture where teamwork is essential. Such schools aspire to be genuine communities of learning.

17. Nurturing the power of the imagination enables learners to (re)construct new symbols and images and discover new possibilities. Imaginative knowing breaks out of the sterile mold of dull conformity and predictability.

18. Learning experiences are heightened when students utilize all possible channels of learning: visual, tactile, auditory, movement, olfactory.

19. Learning can be fun and rewarding.

20. The physical environment is to be friendly to learning.

21. Learning is enhanced when teachers care about and love their students with a genuine interest in them as people and not as educational objects. A climate of mutual respect between people creates a trusting learning environment.

22. The learning process should utilize the wisdom and support of participants in the program, wherever possible. The parent body in any school, for example, constitutes a rich fund of skills, experience, and knowledge (Beare, Caldwell & Millikan, 199). Dialogue with parents about student learning is essential for a cooperative approach to learning between home and school.

23. A teacher needs to make a personal ongoing commitment to learning through reading, in-service study courses, and research. The model of the teacher as enthusiastic learner is not lost on students. A good idea for each teacher is to formulate personal yearly learning goals.

24. Research on adult learning emphasizes the importance of relevance to life situations, an expectation about

participating in learning, the power of motivation, honoring the life experiences of the people, and the value of peer learning.

25.   Finally, the effectiveness of learning is to be regularly evaluated. All teachers have stories similar to the following account of a mother who asked her daughter what she had learned from the Sunday school lesson. The mother was puzzled to hear that her daughter had learned about a cross-eyed bear called Gladly. Only later did it dawn on the mother that the children had been taught the hymn *Gladly the Cross I'd Bear*.

Learning does not happen in a value vacuum. The way we teach and learn is a reflection of what we teachers believe about learning and the values we hold about people. If teachers are to fulfill their role as facilitators of learning, then they must be prepared to involve their students in a process of sharing knowledge, acquiring skills and information, testing out ideas with one another, and consciousness-raising. In this role, they are not the source of all knowledge but fellow travelers on the journey of learning.

Christian Perspectives on Learning

For a Christian, learning is grounded in a worldview that takes its inspiration from the Judeo-Christian heritage. The Christian teacher understands God as Trinity, relational and communal in essence. Trinitarian learning is cooperative and life-giving.

The Christian tradition of education emphasizes the principle of rationality, that is, our God-given reason possesses the capacity for and obligation to expand the boundaries of knowledge and comprehend the natural world. Our intellect is gifted, in cooperation with all living things, to share

in a special way the illumination of divine wisdom in the
universe.

Values described in the gospels provide a religious
framework for learning from a Christian perspective. The
gospel values listed below are relevant to a teacher's own
philosophy of learning.

- caring relationships (Jn 15:1–17)
- inclusion of everybody in the new community (Mk
2: 15–17)
- reverence for people's dignity (Jn 8:1–11)
- everyone has something to give to the community
(Jn 4:7)
- reconciliation with those who have moved away
from the family circle (Lk 15:11–32)
- those who are attentive listeners gain a hundredfold
(Mk 4: 1–9)
- there is a future! (Mk 4:30–32)
- be true to your own beliefs (Mt 6:21)
- be compassionate (Lk 10:29–37)
- it takes some time before we see clearly (Mk 8:25)
- if we fail, why not try again? (Jn 21:17)
- learn through stories and parables (Lk 14:16–24)
- we should seek to model the values we espouse (Mt
5:16)
- discern the way of integrity and expose false illusions of power (Mt 4:1–11)
- take time out to reflect on what is happening (Mk
6:31)
- be prepared to stand up for what you believe in (Mk
6:1–6)
- remember to say thanks for all good things (Lk
10:21–22)

• we can bring light and wisdom to each other (Jn 7:12)

and from the epistles:

• working as a team is fruitful in its outcomes (1 Cor 3:5–9)
• good teaching will utilize the many diverse gifts in the group (1 Cor 12:4–11)
• the spirit of love pervades all good teaching (1 Cor 13)
• don't be discouraged by setbacks and opposition—have courage! (2 Cor 4:7–11)

These New Testament passages present us with a value context for our learning and teaching approaches. The kerygmatic role of the church in its mission of teaching reflects the church's sacred memory of Jesus the Teacher. Learning in the Christian tradition should never be reduced to a series of strategies and techniques. The implementation of values that teachers hold about the sacredness of the human person and learning is a service to the well-being of the planet. Religious learning is an unceasing search for the wisdom of Eternal Truth.

Arrogance is a block to learning. A Zen story tells of a pompous businessman who went to the Zen master for spiritual knowledge. No sooner had they met than the businessman began to boast about his many exploits in commerce. The Zen master eventually interrupted the flow of ego boosting and asked the man if he would like some tea. "Yes," answered the businessman, and then proceeded to continue his account of accumulated wealth. The Zen master began pouring tea until it flooded the floor. The businessman paused and shouted: "Stop! The cup is overflowing!" "So are you," retorted the Zen master, "You will never learn until you empty yourself."

Pressure to conform to fit predetermined molds in education is another inhibiting factor in good learning. Anthony De Mello tells the story of the royal pigeon.

Once upon a time, Nasruddin became prime minister of a distant kingdom. One day when he was wandering about the palace, he spied a royal falcon. He had never seen this variety of pigeon before so he ordered the royal servants to secure the falcon. The falcon's beak, wings, and claws were trimmed with scissors. "Now," said Nasruddin, "you look like a proper royal pigeon. The royal Keeper of the palace has been neglecting you and I will speak severely to him!" (De Mello 1982: 8)

Conclusion

Hard-pressed teachers who struggle to cope with crowded classrooms, diverse problems in the group, disruptive students, and limited resources may look with a jaundiced eye on the ideas explored in this chapter, which may seem far removed from the hurly-burly doings of an ordinary classroom. Although there are formidable constraints to the attainment of a thoughtful classroom faithful to basic principles of learning, teachers might take heart from the advances made in classroom learning approaches over the last decade. Even small modifications to teaching styles may lead to a more participative way of learning. The information revolution is challenging teachers to ensure that computer technology remains firmly the servant, not the master, of how learning is facilitated.

Learning invites teachers to review their ways of teaching

and to align their approaches to learning with their own charter of beliefs about holistic education.

Reflection

1. Think about your own experiences as a learner. Jot down three significant learning times for you.

What was the nature of the learning activities? Why were they effective for you?

What did you learn from them about teaching and learning?

2. What is your preferred way of learning? How best do you learn?

3. Reflect on your teaching activities over the last two weeks. Make a list of the various learning strategies you have used.

Which learning activities seemed to be successful? Why?

What insights do you glean from evaluating your learning strategies?

With your school staff or parish educational team, discuss the twenty-five propositions about the facilitation of learning described in this chapter. Apply each one to learning in your school or educational agency.

4. Dream a little about an ideal learning environment. Imagine the main features of such an environment and record them.

Now visualize your actual learning environment. What one aspect of this environment can you modify to make it more in accord with the ideal situation which you have visualized?

5. If you teach in a school, invite the staff to draw up a charter of beliefs about learning and compose a school statement. Research the Scriptures to support each statement in your charter with a biblical quote or story.

6. Compose your own Credo on learning, starting with the words, "This is what I believe about learning…"

7. There are any number of teaching strategies. Which ones do you use? Which ones do you wish to implement in your methods of teaching?

From discussions with other teachers compile twenty useful teaching strategies. I have listed a few well-known methods below:

• Brainstorm—write down as many as you can think of; don't evaluate them. Just let them flow.

• No repeats—add new ideas when reporting to the group. Don't repeat what has been said already.

• Three-person teach—teacher teaches the concept; students in pairs then teach the concept to each other.

5

JUSTICE

O nce upon a time a fugitive was hiding in a village.
The soldiers came and demanded that the fugitive
be handed over to them. The soldiers said that
unless the villagers did so, they would execute ten hostages.
The villagers went to the religious leader who sought an
answer from his Bible. All day long he stayed in his room
alone, pondering on various passages in his Bible. At last he
came across a passage from the eleventh chapter of the
gospel of John which said that it is right that "one man
should die for the people, rather than that the whole nation
should perish" (Jn 11:50). The religious leader then went
immediately to the soldiers and told the soldiers where the
fugitive was hiding. The fugitive was captured and executed by a firing squad. That night an angel appeared to the
religious leader and reproached him for sending the messiah to his death. The religious leader was aghast and defend-
ed himself by saying that he had prayed from the Bible all
day in his room. But the angel replied: "Instead of praying
from the Bible all day in your room, you should have visit-

ed him and looked him in the eye. Then you would have known he was the messiah."

Those who follow the path of justice act on the belief that every person is our brother or sister and has the right to a life of dignity. A Hindu proverb has a similar theme as the story recounted above.

I looked into the distance and saw something,
I thought it was an animal.
As it came closer I saw it was a man.
And when I stood,
and looked into his eyes,
I saw it was my brother.

We become more attuned to the imperatives of the path of justice when we move from a selfish elitism to a point of solidarity with all humanity and creation. When our perception of people is transformed from categories of race, skin color, religion, or status to one of fellowship, then we can share the joys and anguish of the family of humankind. The subtle temptation for teachers is to categorize students according to intelligence, talent, gender, application, and personality. This kind of stereotyping is just as deadly to the self-esteem of students as categories of race, skin color, and social status. In an ideal world, all teacher and student interactions in the school setting demonstrate a commitment to justice. Teachers encounter many faces of justice in everyday school or parish life. Examples of these would be assessment and evaluation procedures, ethnic sensitivities, responses to students with learning difficulties, equal opportunities for girls and boys to develop skills, the quality of communications with parents, students-at-risk, deprivation, unemployment, racial prejudice.

The path of justice works to restore harmony in creation. Racism, sexism, hunger, political and social oppression are affronts to God's dream for a world without oppression. One senses something of God's dream for a harmonious world in chapter 11 of the book of Isaiah:

> The wolf will live with the lamb.
> the panther lie down with the kid,
> calf, lion and fat-stock beast together
> with a little child to lead them (Is 11:6).

Justice was the spark that ignited the fire of the ministry of Jesus: "I have come to bring fire to the earth, and how I wish it were blazing already" (Lk 12:49). In Luke's gospel, Jesus is portrayed as beginning his public mission with a ringing cry for justice. In his hometown of Nazareth, he enters the synagogue, unrolls the scroll and reads from the text of Isaiah:

> The spirit of the Lord is on me,
> for he has anointed me
> to bring the good news to the afflicted.
> He has sent me to proclaim liberty to captives,
> sight to the blind,
> to let the oppressed go free,
> to proclaim a year of favor from the Lord (Lk 4:18–19).

Teachers and Justice

Injustice appears in many guises. Teachers witness students who are victims of sexual harassment, bullying, racial abuse, and poverty. Teachers have seen those who are denied opportunities to appreciate post-Vatican theology, or are alienated because of an inappropriate curriculum. It hurts teachers to see the impact of financial or emotional deprivation on students. They see people torn apart in family acrimony. Nightly TV newscasts recount a litany of local, national, and global assaults on human dignity and planetary health. Teachers are on the cutting edge of society in the work of educating young people. Dehumanizing forces in the community have an immediate influence on the quality of education.

How do teachers respond to the many manifestations of injustice? One possible response is to throw up one's hands in despair at the enormity of the task and leave it to someone else. Some teachers argue that the forces of injustice are so entrenched in the very fabric of society that their puny efforts will count for nothing. Anyway, they say, schools should not become instruments of political indoctrination. Such teachers might well ponder on the words of Paulo Freire: "Washing one's hands of the conflict between the powerful and the powerless means to side with the powerful and not be neutral." If teachers are not part of the solution, they are part of the problem.

A more creative response to the cries of oppression would insist that schools and teachers can, should, and do make a difference if responsible strategies are developed and implemented. However, teachers and schools should not take upon themselves an exaggerated view of their contribution to the promotion of social justice. The structures of society and ideologies that reinforce inequity and injustice are endemic to our society. Many community agencies and political lobbies will have to work cooperatively to confront areas of injustice. Teachers who are committed to justice will inform themselves about community groups and communicate with such groups to further the cause of justice.

Teachers themselves are influenced by societal attitudes

toward issues of justice that range across the whole spectrum of views, from conservative positions (which endorse the status quo and relegate issues into the "too hard" basket), to those who "tut-tut" about injustice, to a minority who work for radical changes in society. A general way of designating the various approaches to justice can be stated as the "3R's":

Remuneration:
... people get what they deserve; hard work is rewarded, laziness is punished.
Restoration:
... those who are in need should be given generous support.
Reconstruction:
... for justice to happen, the roots of oppression have to be combated; society has to be reconstructed.

Another way of describing attitudes toward the issue of justice would be to identify the three worldviews of conservative, liberal, and radical perspectives. The conservative position says that there are winners and losers in the world—"sorry, but that's the way the cookie crumbles in life!" The liberal view is that we should give maximum support to the disadvantaged; the radical stance is that subversive action is necessary to overturn structures oppressive to human dignity and planetary health. When confronted with unjust situations, people may respond in a variety of ways, such as, "What do you expect from lazy people who just look for handouts!" or "I just don't want to know about it, it's all too much for me, I've got enough to cope with myself!" or "Well, let's start somewhere and do something about it" or "An interesting but sad situation of oppression which calls for more research" or "You never know, maybe the poor are happier than we are."

Working for justice is always going to be a struggle because injustice arises out of an oppressive utilization of power or domination. To transform unjust systems or situations means confronting entrenched interests who will usually fight to retain privilege or power over others. A teacher may have to put up with vituperation and exclusion from power blocs or individuals who are threatened by actions for justice. The issue may be about enrollment policies, school excursions, inclusion policies for disadvantaged students, assessment and reporting procedures, modifications to the curriculum, and teacher workloads. The problem usually lies in transforming hearts toward justice, not just modifying particular structures and policies. Most of us like to retain the comfort of the status quo. My experience is that one of the most painful struggles in working for justice is the battle with my own possessiveness and securities. Often I lack the moral courage to take stands for justice because I fear the consequences of the ensuing conflict.

A Changing Worldview of Justice in the Church

The twentieth century marks a watershed in the way justice is understood in church teaching. The emergence of liberation, creation, and feminist theologies, which have a particular orientation toward justice, provides a solid theological and spiritual underpinning to the church's position on justice. Walter Burghardt, S.J., describes the movement in church teaching from a charity stance to one of solidarity with the poor. He writes:

I find it fascinating that the biblical approach to the poor has found its way into more recent church teach-

ing. You see, in a world that was hierarchically structured (home, school, church, state, society) Leo XIII
and Pius X could not help seeing the poor at the bottom of the economic ladder apparently ordained by
God to remain that way. For Pius XI the poor were
poor because personal sin and selfishness held sway in
the world. Even Pius XII and John XXIII did not challenge the place of the poor within the existing structures of society. But with Paul VI and John Paul II, as
well as documents of the Latin American and North
American bishops, a significant shift took place. Now
the "plight of the poor" is seen not primarily as a part
of reality that calls for charity, but as part of disordered
systems calling for justice. In this context the spirituality demanded is solidarity with the poor (Burghardt,
61).

What a challenge! How does a teacher try to be faithful to
"solidarity with the poor" within the complexity of economic, religious, and social forces that influence the scope
and direction of education?

Liberation theology had its genesis in a Christian
response to the oppressive South and Central American
political and social scene. During the 1960s the desperate
plight of the majority of people who were deprived of their
basic rights provoked theologians to formulate their theology from the inspiration of the Good News as an invitation to
freedom. God is not removed from human history but is
passionately involved in the quest for the "fullness of life"
(Jn 10:10). The exodus is a core symbol for the liberation theologians, signifying as it does the passage from slavery to
freedom. Feminist theology extends the scope of liberation
theology through its focus on gender equity and the affir-

mation of partnership between women and men. The intolerable condition of women in many countries is a violation of justice. Many world religious traditions have unfortunately sanctified demeaning attitudes toward women— "Men are superior to women because of the qualities in which Allah has given their superiority" (Koran); "I give you thanks, O Lord our God, King of the Universe that I was not born a woman" (traditional male Orthodox Jewish prayer); "For man did not come from woman; no, woman came from man; nor was man created for the sake of woman, but woman for the sake of man" (1 Cor 11:8–9). Creation theology is concerned with safeguarding the integrity of creation and linking stewardship with discipleship. These three theologies are gradually entering the mainstream of the life of the church and aspire to implement a vision of a just society.

Approaches to Justice

For a teacher, the quest to promote justice can involve a whole range of diverse activities and approaches. There are at least five features of a just teacher. She or he would:

- be a truthful person;
- support movements for justice;
- reverence life and be a hopeful presence;
- be critically aware of oppressive situations;
- be a practitioner of just processes.

The movement toward justice might be described in four phases:

- attending to what is going on, becoming aware of the oppression;

- a critical analysis of the forces of oppression;
- asserting oneself with others for the cause of justice;
- participating in appropriate action.

For justice to happen we must start somewhere.

Start Somewhere

A real threat to pursuing a course of justice is to succumb to the "paralysis by analysis" syndrome. This condition can occur when a person becomes overwhelmed by the sea of trauma in the world. As horror story after horror story multiplies, a sensitive teacher can feel that the concerns for justice become impossible mountains to climb. A very appropriate story to combat the feeling of powerlessness is the story of "One at a Time."

Once upon a time a visitor was strolling along a beach in Mexico when he noticed a local person walking slowly toward him picking up starfish which had been washed ashore. He then threw them back into the sea, rather than let them die from being beached. The visitor said to the local person, "I admire what you are doing but there are thousands of dying starfish on the beach. Can't you see that you are not really making a difference to these thousands of starfish?" At this the local person picked up a starfish and flung it back into the sea saying, "Well, I've made a difference to this one!" (Canfield & Hansen: 22-23).

The story reminds me of Mother Teresa's famous dictum to her Sisters who daily face a multitude of suffering and dying people, "Sisters don't think of the masses but one by one by one."

Teachers need to avoid presenting their students with a litany of depressing stories about hunger, unemployment, war, ecological vandalism, violence, and crime. These litanies simply reinforce the view that the poor are powerless. Why not encourage students to become involved for justice by telling stories of resistance where courageous people confronted injustice and won? The Christian story is founded on the wondrous belief that God so loved the world that God sent his Son who overcame suffering and death through his resurrection. Good eventually will triumph. There were probably thousands of lepers in Palestine in the time of Jesus, but he cured only a very small number of them. Teachers can only do what they can do.

Relevance

Most of us find it difficult to become actively involved in faraway concerns except for contributions to famine or disaster appeals. Teachers may find it more meaningful for their students to address issues of justice that impact on students' lives. Students may be anxious about employment and need to understand unemployment; they may be experiencing harassment, bullying, sexism; their families may be in financial hardship. Students may be embarrassed by the cost of school excursions or school uniforms; they may feel that the curriculum is not relevant to their aspirations. Action for justice will focus on an immediate and relevant concern and will, at the same time, help students to see the interconnectedness of the various forms of injustice which ultimately express an unequal distribution of power.

Students can be empowered to acquire ways of challenging the unequal distribution of power by engaging in a process conducive to promoting justice. According to a Social Justice Research Group in Adelaide, Australia, there are three major phases of such a process. These three phases are:

- consciousness-raising to become more aware of the dynamics of the unjust situation;
- contact with groups in the community who are involved in like-minded activities;
- initiate or support appropriate social action to alleviate the oppression (Education for Social Justice Research Group, 26).

Again, I would emphasize the importance of stressing the telling of stories of the resistance rather than the oppressed—not just about the Holocaust but of Jewish resistance to Nazi tyranny; not just about the poverty of many minority groups but examples of resistance struggles.

Critical Analysis and Skills

Students are taught skills in critical analysis, the gathering of information on a topic, methods of critiquing the data on an issue of injustice, generating alternative ways of functioning, and learning to uncover and evaluate their own prejudices. Field experiences raise student awareness about the reality of injustice. A prayerful discernment of concerns helps ground the process of critical analysis in the spirit of Christ. Students also need to learn how the cause of social justice is furthered by skills of engagement. These skills include the art of writing on concerns of justice; how to communicate with influential groups who may be able to facilitate action; where resources may be found; and how best to articulate a coherent and well informed point of view. Curriculum areas such as social studies, home economics, legal studies, science, language arts, and multicultural programs offer many opportunities for raising justice questions. Skills in conflict management enable students to deal more effectively with oppression and injustice. Negotiations with community action and awareness groups translate theory into practice. (Who knows how may prisoners have been spared as a result of students' work on behalf of Amnesty International?)

Spirituality

The cause of social justice is enhanced when action for justice is firmly anchored in a vibrant spirituality that honors human dignity and creation as fashioned in God's likeness. Such a spirituality is characterized by a generous self-giving without any expectation of reward or recognition. A teacher's hopeful and healing presence will reflect some of the passionate longing of Jesus' ministry for justice. Two other features mark such a spirituality. The first is that its reality does not exist in remote rooms of theological towers but in the marketplace of hunger, violence, unemployment, and other forms of oppression. The other feature is that it is a spirituality of action expressed in the struggles and turmoil of seeking to overcome obstacles to human dignity. Action for justice is not patronage but solidarity. As Lilla Watson, an Aboriginal worker for justice, once said: "If you've come to help me, you are wasting your time. But if you have come because your liberation is bound up with mine, then let us work together."

The eucharist is a dramatic symbol for justice. Here is sacred bread for the whole world. The four movements in the story of the institution of the eucharist are four phases of action for justice. Jesus "took some bread," "said the blessing," "he broke it," and "gave it to them" (Mk 14:22; Mt 26:26). We gather bread (a symbol of life), we recall the providential care of God, we divide and share. The miracle of loaves and fishes (Mk 6:30–44) teaches us about the abundance of the earth's resources if we take the risk of sharing them.

Teachers and Work

A teacher spends most of her or his waking hours involved in some kind of paid or unpaid work. What is your attitude toward work? For a Christian, work is not simply an activity for making money to support a particular life-style and further one's career but an act of cocreation in partnership with God's ongoing creativity. The Creator did not adopt an exclusive role in creation but invited humankind into a participative role of stewardship (Gn 2:5–25). Our work can sustain or hinder the cause of justice. The work of good teachers in providing holistic education is precious to the well-being of our world. Teachers know that if the future world is to be a more just place, then their students must feel that they have a say in its values and structures. If students experience a sense of dignity in what they do and are empowered to change society, then they are more inclined to value work for its own sake and not merely for its material rewards. The impact of science and technology is a major influence in the lives of students. The work of technology and science is shaping our life-styles and values. Is this work friendly or hostile to planetary health?

A teacher's approach to work is an indicator of what values the teacher considers important. If teachers demonstrate an appreciation of work as a cooperative venture with others, they may communicate something of the dignity of work as community service as well as a means of livelihood. As a teacher of many years, I see my work as sharing the accumulated wisdom of the human spirit. I hope that my teaching endeavors in various countries contribute to the liberation of people through learning and a religious celebration of life. Our work is a part of the larger global reality, but we must learn to focus on the immediate needs of our local situation. Our challenge is to see each small action we make as part of a global movement for change in a better world. Creative teaching does make a difference to the cause of justice. If even one of our students becomes more involved in working for justice, our teaching has borne fruit.

It's a real thrill to witness graduates of our teaching who make real contributions to society. I believe it's one of the special rewards of teaching.

We can discover God's presence in our daily work at home and in teaching. Holiness is to be found in the mundane doings of the schoolyard, grocery shopping, classroom teaching, attending to a sick child, or driving the kids to band practice. The story of Jesus and work is salutary. Most of his working life was occupied not in teaching and healing, but in the obscure labor of a carpenter around Nazareth. Anthony De Mello tells a story to illustrate this theme.

> Once upon a time, a businessman went to the Master for spiritual guidance. The Master said: "As the fish perishes on dry land, so you perish when you get entangled in the world. The fish must return to the water and you must return to solitude." The businessman was very upset. "Must I give up my business and go into a monastery?"
>
> "Of course not," said the Master, "hold on to your business but go into your heart" (De Mello 1986, 13).

This story reminds us that solitude is inseparable from productive work. The climax of the creation story is not the creation of people on the "sixth day" but the time of sabbath when the work of creation was celebrated as "very good" by a contemplative God. A teacher's creative energies become exhausted without the recovering gift of sabbath. Sabbath slows down the pace of the fast-food culture and unplugs the Walkman. Sabbath silence is not a sterile cessation of noise but a savoring of the wonder and mystery of creation. Nor is the scholastic experience a retreat from the world simply to be refreshed, but an invitation to rediscover spiritual truths that empower teachers to act decisively on their responses to a host of clamoring voices.

Teachers and the Earth Community

If the work of justice is to restore harmony within the integrity of creation, then a teacher's role in this movement is vital. Although the Judeo-Christian story insists that the divine covenant is between God, us, and the earth (Gn 9), an obsessive anthropocentrism in church teaching limited the scope of covenant relationships to God and humankind. Until very recently, the church was blind to ethical issues of the environment. Public church teachings on our relationships with creation were virtually nonexistent. As late as 1967, *Populorum Progressio*, the church's charter for development, stated that, "By persistent work and use of his intelligence, man wrests nature's secrets from her and finds a better application for her riches" (n. 25). To be fair, the church's teachings reflected a general community view of anthropocentrism which held that human beings could do what they liked with nature.

During the last quarter of the twentieth century, there has been a growing awareness of the church's responsibility to be an active moral agent in earth care ethics. Mainline Protestant churches in the World Council of Churches gatherings in Vancouver, Basel, Seoul, and Canberra have insisted that ecology is a fundamental dimension of justice and peace. With Jeremiah we cry out, "How long will the land be in mourning, and the grass wither all over the countryside? The animals and the birds are dying as a result of the wickedness of the inhabitants" (Jer 12:4).

Although ecological concerns such as ozone layer depletion, salinity, deforestation, global warming, and pollution are common topics of public debates and research, the economic and political forces driving ecological devastation are not always understood. Western industrialized countries are consuming the earth's resources at an alarming rate. Structural ecological pillage that results when affluent western countries place an economic stranglehold on poorer countries is difficult for the average person to comprehend. We must not only address questions of sustainable economies but sustainable life-styles. Donal Dorr writes:

> The people at the top of the pyramids of power are the ones who must be held mainly accountable for structural injustice; for they are the ones who could most easily change the system. But they are the people least likely to replace the unjust structures, since they have most to lose (Dorr, 60).

Teachers can do much to advance the cause of justice and earth care. Their own love of the earth and care with its resources will certainly impress students. The school curriculum embraces many aspects of earth care. We come as humble learners to the first people of our respective countries and discover the power of their belief in the essential unity of creation. School projects about earth care, forest excursions, environment-friendly school grounds, family involvement in ecology, and parish and school celebrations of the blessings of creation are just some examples of how we can all learn to contribute to the healing of the earth. It is quite extraordinary to consider that not a single liturgical feast in the entire church calendar celebrates creation. Let our students believe in the prospect of recovery where the earth can be regenerated, if we become truly reconciled to each other and to the earth. Our vision for justice is not only about the good of humankind but the well-being of the planet. We need to re-imagine the styles and practices of living within the well-being of planetary health. The earth is our companion. After all, when we really think about it, Christianity is truly a materialist religion because its core doctrine of the Incarnation insists that all matter is ultimately holy.

Conclusion

Justice speaks of a teacher's vision for a world where we learn to live with reverence and simplicity within the intricate and fragile network of creation. Teachers choose this path when they strive to be just in their relationships and educate students into both the awareness of oppression and the skills to bring about a more just world.

Reflection

1. Who are your heroines and heroes in struggles for justice?

What qualities do you admire in these people?

2. Identify a situation of injustice that impacts on you now.

What are your feelings about this situation?

What is your response to the situation?

Specify the forces that are causing this situation of injustice.

3. Tell the story of your search for justice.

Who influenced your story?

What event(s) have modified your worldview about justice issues?

4. Is your school or parish a just place? Analyze the just and unjust features of the life of the school or parish.

5. Research the Bible to discover your favorite stories and sayings about justice.

6. Consider these topics as they relate to social justice and fill in the chart below:

Topic of social justice	Implications for teaching	Elaboration of issues
curriculum		
ecology		
racism		
poverty		
unemployment		
school policies		
sexism		
bullying		

7. Compose a charter of basic rights for:

Staff members
Students
Parents
Members of the parish community

EPILOGUE

The five dimensions of teaching—integrity, wisdom, generativity, learning, and justice—converge in a holistic vision and practice of good teaching. But teaching can be a perilous as well as a satisfying vocation because each dimension has its shadow. To sustain a vision, teachers must be aware of these shadows and deal courageously with them. The shadow of integrity is duplicity, for wisdom it is foolishness, for generativity it is sterility, for learning it is closure, and for justice the shadow is oppression. A healthy regard for the power of each shadow will help teachers avoid the pitfalls.

Teaching is much more than instruction. It is a service to enlarge the community's heritage of wisdom and to empower people to realize the gifts they possess. Good teaching nudges students to open up new horizons of possibilities. Christopher Logue has expressed this pushing and nudging of students to try new things in a dialogue:

"Come to the edge"
We might fall.
"Come to the edge"
It's too high!
COME TO THE EDGE
And they came.
And he pushed,
And they flew (Logue, 96).

By helping students to risk flying, teachers engage in the prophetic dimension of teaching. Our students are invited to re-imagine a new world order and acquire a new openness toward reality. In the words of Teilhard, "To understand the world, knowledge is not enough. You must see it, touch it, live in its presence and drink the vital heat of existence in the very heart of reality." This sense of openness to reality breaks out from the confines of a pragmatic and functional view of world. It evokes surprise at the depth and height of God's gracious love in creation.

The five essential qualities of teaching lead teachers and students into sharing some of the mystery and wonder of this love. Finally, this convergence happens when one is prepared to allow the Spirit to emerge out of our ordinary endeavors. Teilhard has the last word: "We spend our lives waiting for the great day, the great battle, or the great deed of power. But that external consummation is not given to many, nor is it necessary. So long as our being is tensed passionately into the spirit in everything, then that spirit will emerge from our hidden, nameless efforts."

As teachers let us be "tensed passionately into the spirit in everything"!

Process

To assist you and your teaching group to process the five paths of teaching, three approaches are suggested below. You may wish to adapt them to your local situation or personal needs.

1. REAP

The law of the harvest says you reap what you sow.

R ead and research a chapter or section of this book.

E xplore and evaluate the theme of the chapter.

A pply the theme to one's life.

P lan for the future.

2. PEER TEACHING

With a peer companion, select two topics from one of the chapters, for example, features of a thoughtful classroom, teachers as facilitators of learning. Each person in the dyad spends some time studying the topic and then teaches the topic to the peer companion.

3. CIRCLE LEARNING

The group sits in a circle. Each person selects a section of a chapter, reflectively reads this section, and then in turn, around the circle, explains to the people in the learning circle what this section means to her or his experience of teaching.

BIBLIOGRAPHY

Beare, H., B.J. Caldwell, and R.H. Millikan, *Creating an Excellent School—Some New Management Techniques*. London: Routledge.

Birch, C. 1990. *On Purpose*. Sydney: NSW University Press, Ltd.

Burghardt, W., SJ. *Characteristics of Social Justice Spirituality*, Origins, July 21, 1994, Vol. 24, No. 9.

Canfield, J. & M.V. Hansen. 1993. *Chicken Soup for the Soul—101 Stories to Open the Heart and Rekindle the Spirit*. Deerfield Park, SL: Health Communications Inc.

Covey, S. R. 1990. *The Seven Habits of Highly Effective People*. Melbourne: The Business Library.

De Bono, E. 1985. *Six Thinking Hats—The Power of Focused Thinking*. New York: International Center for Creative Thinking.

De Chardin, T. 1964. *Le Milieu Divin*. London: Fontana.

De Mello, A. 1982. *The Song of the Bird*. Anand, India: Gusarat-Sahitya Prakash.

De Mello, A. 1983. *One Minute Wisdom*. Garden City, NY: Doubleday.

Dorr, D. 1984. *Spirituality and Justice*. Dublin: Gill and Macmillan.

Education for Social Justice Research Group. 1994. *Teaching for Resistance*. Adelaide: Centre for Studies in Educational Leadership.

Edwards, D. 1995. *Jesus The Wisdom of God: An Ecological Theology*. Homebush, N.S.W.: St. Paul's.

Glasser, W. 1990. *The Quality School—Managing Students without Coercion*. New York: Perennial Library, Harper and Row.

Goleman, D. 1995. *Emotional Intelligence*. New York: Bantam Books.

Horsfield, P. *Religious Beliefs and the Communications Media*. Zadok Series 1 Paper, June 1991.

Logue, C. 1981. *Ode to the Dodo: Poems from 1953 to 1978*. London: Jonathan Cape (adapted text).

Lortie, D. 1975. *School Teacher: A Sociological Study: Chicago*. Chicago: University of Chicago Press.

O'Murchu, D. 1987. *Coping with Change in the Modern World*. Dublin: The Mercier Press.

Udall, A.J. & J.E. Daniels. 1991. *Creating Thoughtful Classrooms—Strategies to Promote Student Thinking*. Australia: Hawker Brownlow Education.

Warren, M., "The Electronic Imagined World" in *Religious Education*, Vol. 83, No. 3, Summer 1988.

White, R. "Questionable Assumptions Underlying Secondary School Classrooms" in *Australian Journal of Education*, Vol. 32, No. 3, 1988.

Whitehead, E. Eaton and James D. 1994. *A Sense of Sexuality, Christian Love and Intimacy*. New York: Crossroad.

Whitehead, J.D. and Evelyn Eaton Whitehead. 1996.

Shadows of the Heart: A Spirituality of the Painful Emotions. New York: Crossroad.

Selected Bibliography

In writing this book, I have found the following books useful references and I wish to acknowledge my gratitude for the insights gleaned from these resources.

Balson, M. 1982. *Understanding Classroom Behaviour.* The Australian Council of Educational Research Ltd.

Barclay, W. 1963. *The Plain Man Looks at the Beatitudes.* London: Fontana Books.

Beare, H., B.J. Caldwell, and R.H. Millikan. *Creating an Excellent School—Some New Management Techniques.* London: Routledge.

Bellah, R. et al. 1986. *Habits of the Heart—Individualism and Commitment in American Life.* New York: Harper and Row.

Bellanca, J. & R. Fogarty. 1991. *Blueprint for Thinking in a Cooperative Classroom.* Australia: Hawker Brownlow Education.

Berry, T. with T. Clarke. 1991. *Befriending the Earth—A Theology of Reconciliation between Humans and the Earth.* Mystic, CT: Twenty-Third Publications.

Biggs, J. B. (ed.). 1991. *Teaching for Learning—A View from Cognitive Psychology.* Victoria: ACER.

Collins, P. 1991. *Intimacy and the Hungers of the Heart.* Mystic, CT: Twenty-Third Publications.

Collins, P. 1995. *God's Earth Religion—as if Matter Really Mattered.* North Blackburn Vic.: Harper-Collins.

De Bono, E. 1985. *Six Thinking Hats.* New York: The International Center for Creative Thinking.

Dorr, D. 1984. *Spirituality and Justice.* Dublin: Gill and Macmillan.

Fullan, M. 1993. *Change Forces.* London: Falmer Press.

Gaarder, J. 1995. *Sophie's World—An Adventure in Philosophy.* London: Phoenix House.

Grassi, J.A. 1976. *Jesus as Teacher—A New Testament Guide to Learning the Way.* Winona, MN: St. Mary's College Press.

Grenier, B. 1995. *Jesus the Teacher.* Homebush, N.S.W.: St. Paul's.

Harris, M. 1987. *Teaching and Religious Imagination.* San Francisco: Harper and Row.

Holt, J. 1964. *How Children Fail.* New York: Pitman.

Illich, I. *Deschooling Society.* New York: Harper and Row.

Johnson, E. A. 1993. *She Who Is—the Mystery of God in Feminist Theological Discourse.* New York: Crossroad.

Jones, V.F. and L.S. Jones. 1990. *Comprehensive Classroom Management—Motivating and Managing Students.* Boston: Allyn and Bacon.

Lang, G. and C. Berberich. 1995. *All Children are Special—Creating an Inclusive Classroom.* Armadale, Vic.: Eleanor Curtin Pub.

Lazear, D. 1991. *Seven Ways of Teaching—The Artistry of Teaching with Multiple Intelligencies.* Australia: Hawker Brownlow Education.

Marks, L. 1989. *Living with Vision—Reclaiming the Power of the Heart.* Indiana: Knowledge Systems Inc.

McKinney, M.B. 1987. *Sharing Wisdom, A Process for Group Decision Making.* Texas: Tabor.

Moore, T. 1992. *Care for the Soul—A Guide for Cultivating Depth and Sacredness in Everyday Life.* New York: HarperCollins.

O'Donoghue, M., B. Moore, N. Habel, R. Crotty, M. Crotty. 1993. *Social Justice in Today's World—Finding a Just Way.* Melbourne: Collins Dove.

Richo, D. 1991. *How to be an Adult—A Handbook on Psychological and Spiritual Integration.* New York: Paulist.

Sergiovanni, T. J. 1994. *Building Community in Schools.* San Francisco: Jossey-Bass Publications.

Shor, I. 1992. *Empowering Education—Critical Teaching for Social Change.* Chicago: The University of Chicago Press.

Social Justice Research Group. 1994. *Teaching for Resistance—Report of the Education for Social Justice Research Project.* Adelaide: The Centre for Studies in Educational Leadership.

Tarnas, R. 1991. *The Passion of the Western Mind: Understanding the Ideas That Have Shaped Our World View.* New York: Ballantine Books.

Udall, A. J. and J.E. Daniels. 1991. *Creating a Thoughtful Classroom—Strategies to Promote Student Thinking.* Australia: Hawker Brownlow Education.

Whitehead, J. D. and Evelyn Eaton Whitehead. 1980. *Method in Ministry—Theological Reflection and Christian Ministry.* New York: The Seabury Press.

Of Related Interest...

Creative Christian Leadership
Skills for More Effective Ministry
Kevin Treston

Helps Christians in a leadership position, church or other-wise,improve their managerial ability, develop a sense of purpose and reach personal and group goals more effectively. Treston pulls together wisdom from specialists in psychology, sociology and management, mixing their theories with an essential spirituality to guide successful leaders in the coming decades.

ISBN:089622-648-4, 100 pp, $12.95 (order M-54)

A New Vision of Religious Education
Kevin Treston
Foreword by Thomas H. Groome

The author offers practical, straightforward guidance and techniques in this resource book for catechists, adult formation leaders and Catholic school teachers. Highly recommended as the text for catechist formation classes.

ISBN: 0-89622- 558-5, 128 pp, $12.95 (order W-39)

Teaching is Like...
Peeling Back Eggshells
Melannie Svoboda

In this book, Sister Melannie offers some 50 brief reflections that are intended to sustain enthusiasm, bolster morale, and encourage teaching as a grace-filled privilege.

ISBN: 0-89622-613-1, 120 pp, $7.95 (M-06)

Available at religious bookstores or from:

TWENTY-THIRD PUBLICATIONS
P.O. Box 180 • Mystic, CT 06355

For a complete list of quality books and videos call:
1-800-321-0411